IMAGES
of America
SALEM, NH
VOLUME II
TROLLEYS, CANOBIE LAKE,
AND ROCKINGHAM PARK

Trolleys like car No. 144, shown here in 1916, brought thousands of people to Salem to attend Canobie Lake Park and Rockingham Park. Everything from Royal Baking Powder to the *Literary Digest* was advertised on the signs above the seats.

Front Cover Illustration: Massachusetts Northeastern Car No. 90 paused at Point A Station off Raymond Avenue, *c.* 1910. Passengers would soon board the trolley for the last leg of their journey to Canobie Lake Park. The complete photo can be seen on p. 23.

SALEM, NH

VOLUME II

TROLLEYS, CANOBIE LAKE, AND ROCKINGHAM PARK

Douglas Seed and Katherine Khalife

First published 1996

ISBN 0-7524-0438-5

Published by Arcadia Publishing,
an imprint of the Chalford Publishing Corporation
One Washington Center, Dover, New Hampshire 03820
Printed in Great Britain

Library of Congress Cataloging-in-Publication Data applied for

This beautiful, nineteenth-century carousel, now believed to be the oldest one of its type in New England, has been a hallmark of Canobie Lake Park for nearly one hundred years.

Contents

Rockingham Park jockeys paused on August 17, 1948 to read about the death of baseball star Babe Ruth the night before.

Introduction

On the morning of August 25, 1902, everyone, it seemed, was waiting. Salem farmers were waiting for rain. Lawrence, the Massachusetts textile city five miles to the south, was waiting for President Teddy Roosevelt's visit the next day. And up at Canobie Lake Park, trolley company officials were waiting, too. The park was having its opening ceremonies that day, as soon as a trolley-load of VIPs arrived from Lawrence.

Meanwhile, down at Hampshire and Essex Streets, the influential group boarded for its thirty-eight minute excursion to Salem. The trolley headed up Hampshire Street, then onto Broadway in Methuen near Brown Street, turning left again onto Oakland Avenue. After an immediate right turn to Railroad Square, it then whizzed out Pelham Street. Just past Cross Street, the car turned off the Pelham Street line for its five-mile run to Canobie Lake. Now in open country on private rights of way, the motorman was free to make up time he had lost in the city. And make it up he did.

As the tracks crossed Brady Avenue in Salem, they began a downhill, one-mile straightaway, allowing the trolley to travel as fast as its wheels could turn. The contingent of businessmen and politicians held onto their straw hats as the open car sped along at over thirty-five miles per hour. When it passed the twin pine trees near Lowell Road, the motorman slowed to a more reasonable speed for the final leg of the journey.

Finally arriving at Canobie's trolley loop, the guests stepped off. Their hosts escorted them to the Japanese Theater for a vaudeville show, then on to the Ping-Pong building, where tables had been prepared for lunch. At the bountiful meal's conclusion, opening ceremonies got underway. When the speeches had all been given, Lawrence Mayor James F. Leonard rose to give a whistling solo of "Because I Love You." The crowd promptly demanded an encore. The trolley company's new park was now officially open.

Less than eight weeks before, at about 6 am on July 2, Salem had wakened to the clang of its first trolley bell. Nobody knew it at the time, but that bell signaled the beginning of a new role for the town. For the rest of the twentieth century Salem would be the playground in Massachusetts' back yard. Trolleys would change Salem, just as they had changed towns all over America.

At the end of the nineteenth century, a nationwide frenzy had been underway. Thousands of tiny companies competed for government sanctions to connect towns and cities with the exciting new technology of interurban electric trolleys. By 1900, the United States was honeycombed with 15,000 miles of trolley track carrying over 30,000 cars—quite an achievement in a country with only 8,000 miles of paved roads.

Unlike traditional railroads with their long, heavy coaches and fuel-hungry, water-thirsty locomotives, streetcars were small, self-powered marvels whose tight turning radii allowed them to go most anywhere that rights of way could be acquired. The rapid spread of trolley systems brought a previously unknown freedom of travel to the American working class. For those living in small towns like Salem, a ride to the beach or an afternoon of shopping in the city was now not only possible but also easy, quick, and inexpensive. For city dwellers like those in Lawrence—many of whom had never been able to venture much beyond their own crowded tenement districts—the electric roads meant that afternoons of fresh air and open space were now just a nickel or a dime away. And to country and city folks alike, trolleys brought another phenomenon as well—the thrills and excitement of the amusement parks built on their lines.

By the turn of the century, almost every city in the country had a trolley park at its edge, shrewdly constructed by a streetcar company to attract summer and weekend riders. New England certainly had its share: Riverside, Whalom, Pine Island, Norumbega, and Lakeview Parks were only a few of the trolley properties that abounded here. Some were not much more than a picnic grove and a dance board; others possessed wonders enough to stagger even the wildest imagination.

Whatever their facilities, trolley parks were most importantly a place to *go*—in an age when going places was a relatively new concept for many Americans. With sixty-hour workweeks still the norm—and recent immigrants still toiling feverishly to grab even a low rung on the economic ladder—the parks offered accessible recreation on a scale unheard of before.

When the electric road finally stretched itself to the shores of Canobie Lake in 1902, the jam-packed trolleys arriving at the park brought only the first of millions who would eventually travel to Salem for recreation and enjoyment.

Three years later, in 1905, the B&M railroad deposited two famous millionaire speculators on Salem's doorstep. They were looking for an out of the way place to build a race track, far away from the glare of big government attention.

Thirty years earlier they wouldn't have needed to worry about any glare. In the decades after the Civil War, over 300 horse racing tracks had sprung up around the United States. Not surprisingly, though, book makers, gangsters and crooked politicians soon corrupted the industry, and state after state began passing anti-gambling laws. By the time the two millionaires got off the train in Salem, race tracks were being shut down at a dizzying pace. There were only a few dozen left in the whole country.

The two financiers figured they were home free when they saw Salem. Certainly no one would bother them here, in a little country town, in a little rural state whose total population amounted to less than two-thirds the population of Boston. Yes, this was the place. So, the next year, another trolley brought another Lawrence mayor to Salem, this time for the grand opening of Rockingham Park. It's good that he came when he did. The little rural state was about to shut the place down.

For the next twenty-five years Rockingham saw only occasional activity. It would be 1931 before a Russian-American boxing promoter-turned raincoat manufacturer would come on the scene to give it the life it was built for. By then, the trolleys which had sprung up so quickly to revolutionize America had all but disappeared, made obsolete by the Model-T. Canobie Lake Park had closed in 1929 as a result, but it was about to be rescued, too. As neighboring towns wrestled with the depression, Salem residents actually *found* jobs—preparing both establishments for their grand reopenings.

It's said that timing is everything and, for both Canobie and Rockingham, the time was finally right. Over the next few decades, millions of people would pass through their gates—among them, a parade of Hollywood and music industry superstars. Salem would grow up—maybe not in the right direction, according to some people, but grow up nevertheless.

This photo history of Salem trolleys, Canobie Lake, and Rockingham Park is the largest ever done. We hope you'll enjoy it!

Katherine Khalife and Douglas Seed, June 1996

One

Trolleys Come to Town

Salem's trolley era had its beginnings in 1899 when Charles Barnes, an experienced trolley man from Malden, Massachusetts, came up with a proposal to build streetcar lines linking Haverhill, Lawrence, and Nashua. As plans got underway, the Salem shore of Canobie Lake was chosen as the site of the system's amusement park—a necessary feature if the new lines were to attract the heavy ridership required to make them profitable. By late 1900, with companies formed, routes laid out, and government approvals obtained, construction of the lines began. By July of 1902 trolleys like this one would be rolling through Salem.

The Hudson, Pelham & Salem Electric Railway became the operating company of the new venture, which also included the Lawrence & Methuen and the Haverhill & Southern New Hampshire Street Railways. Out of money in 1901, Barnes transferred his interests to Wallace D. Lovell who proposed three more routes and an additional company, the Lowell & Pelham. While all of this was going on at the corporate level during 1901 and 1902, track gangs worked feverishly to construct the system's roadbed, track, and "overhead."

Built to high-quality standards, the road consisted primarily of chestnut ties set on 2-foot centers, with 60 and 70-pound T-Rail in rural areas and 90-pound rail in the cities. Curves were banked for optimum operation at high speeds. By September of 1903, the hearty workers had completed almost 53 miles of track. More than twenty of those miles traveled cross-country over private rights of way.

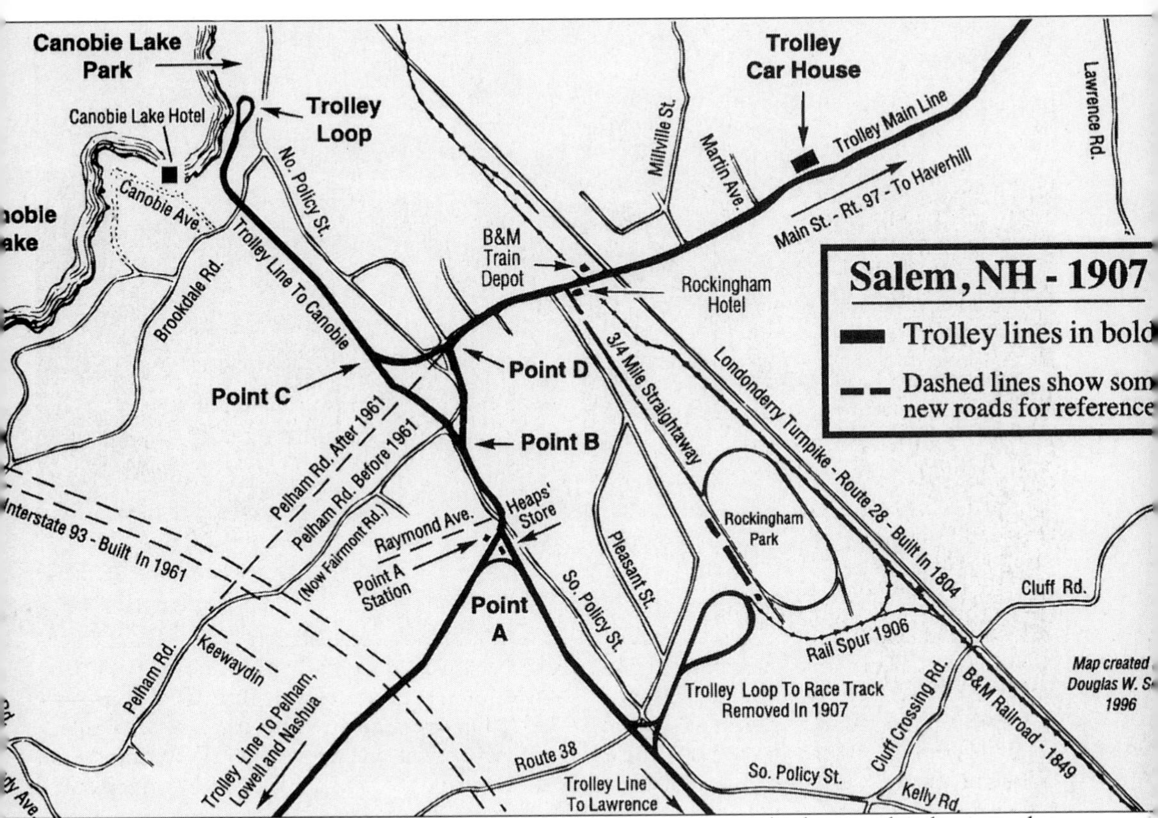

By 1913, the H. P. & S., along with several other small companies, had merged to become the Massachusetts Northeastern Street Railway. Salem—with its key location on the main line between Haverhill and Nashua—was a hub in the company's system and a center of trolley activity and infrastructure.

Operations centered at a huge interchange known as Point A, just west of today's intersection of South Policy Street and Raymond Avenue. From there, the steel ribbons of the company's Salem Division stretched north to Canobie Lake Park, south to Lawrence, west to Nashua, and east over Route 97 to Haverhill.

Since Point A was one-half mile south of the Route 97 main line and streetcars approached it from four different directions, three smaller interchanges—Points B, C, and D—were also needed to accomplish orderly operations. Points B and D provided the main line connection between Point A and Route 97. Point C allowed cars from Haverhill to go to and from Canobie without traveling south to Point A.

Trolley rails were laid to service the new race track in 1906, but when the racing venture failed, the tracks were removed. The Boston & Maine Railroad also installed a spur to the track that year, entering Rockingham south of the oval.

Dashed lines indicating new and relocated roads are included on this map to assist the reader in understanding the exact locations of the features shown.

The heart of the system was the Salem Carhouse, which still sits today on the north side of Main Street between Park Avenue and Dunbar Terrace. Completed in the summer of 1902, this amazing facility housed virtually all the needs of the railroad–everything from a paint shop to a brass foundry was within its 12-inch-thick brick walls. The building was fully fire protected, first by a sprinkler system fed from the 50,000-gallon water tank shown above, and later from the town water supply.

Nicknamed "Evelyn Nesbith," car No. 80 was caught resting in front of the Salem Carhouse in 1908. Behind her, Main Street stretches toward Salem Depot. A motorman and conductor were assigned to each car until the late 1920s, when declining revenues dictated a change to one-man operations. In 1903, motormen and conductors were paid 20¢ per hour; by 1920 their rates had tripled to 60¢—or $5.40 for a nine-hour day.

The original order for passenger cars was awarded to the Laconia, New Hampshire Car Company. Of the fifty-five ordered, twenty-two were 25- or 30-foot closed cars, and thirty-three were fourteen-bench open cars for anticipated heavy ridership during the summer. One of the fourteen-bench open cars, No. 89, is shown above, on the right. The vehicle to its left was one of a number of work cars used to perform maintenance chores along the lines.

The interior of the Salem Carhouse was so large that it could hold thirty-six cars at one time. On the day this photograph was taken, a variety of open and closed cars waited their turn for service, cleaning, repair, or call to duty. The work pits in the floor allowed the undersides of cars to be easily accessed for servicing.

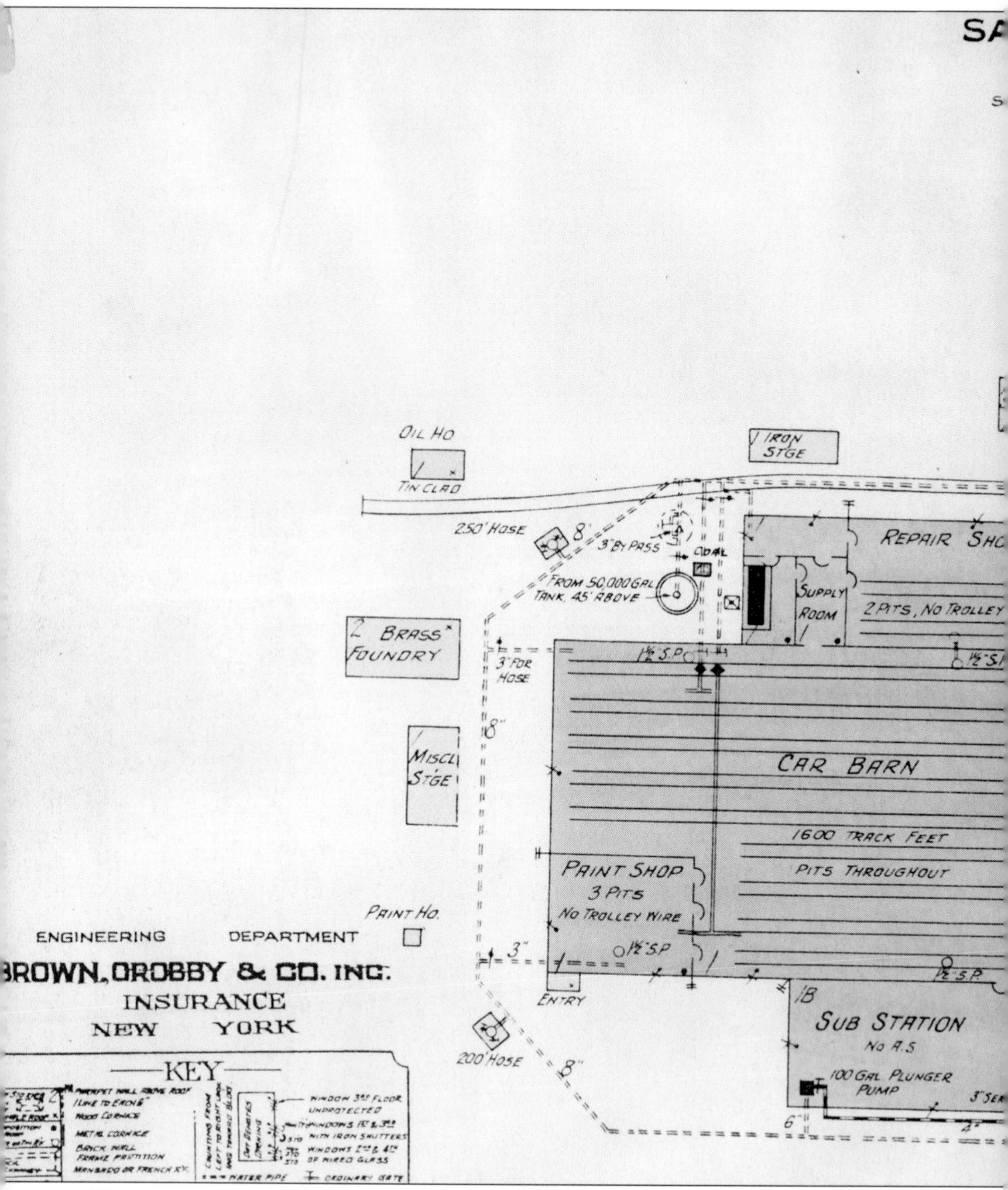

The monstrous Salem Carhouse is detailed in this 1925 insurance company drawing. The primary building was 115 feet wide by 180 feet deep. Its nine tracks could hold a total of thirty-six cars. Attached to the east end of the carbarn was a large repair shop, 45 feet wide and 115 feet long, which could handle an additional four cars. On the west side was a 45-foot by 95-foot, two-story annex containing the division's electrical substation and offices.

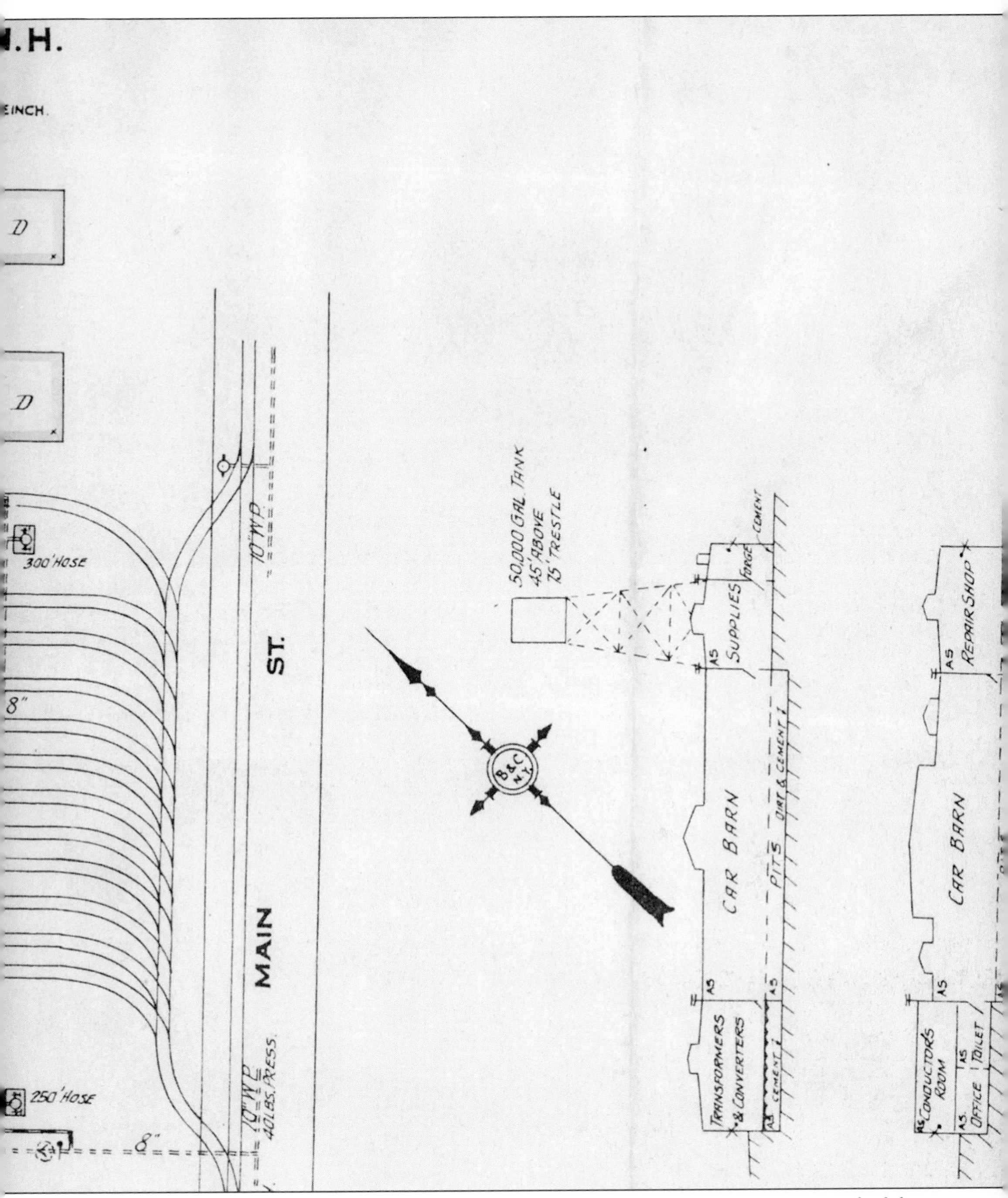

A twelfth track, used to store cars waiting for major repairs, ran down the entire east end of the building. Badly damaged or decrepit, unsaleable cars were burned here, their steel salvaged. The plant provided every trade necessary to keep the line running efficiently. There were paint, carpentry, blacksmith, and machine shops, a brass foundry, a lathe for turning wheels, and a large wheel press. An armature and winding room maintained motors, controllers, and other electrical equipment.

The trolley company was one of Salem's largest employers, with a carbarn crew numbering some forty to fifty men through the second decade of operations. By the mid to late 1920s, however, business was down and the staff was reduced considerably. Upkeep of the lines and rolling stock suffered proportionately. Above, these men have their day's work laid out: repairing and repainting rotating destination box signs, sanding and varnishing woodwork, replacing broken windows, and doing whatever else is required to keep this car rolling and in good order.

Since the company relied on local labor whenever possible, the carbarn workers seen here represent many familiar old Salem families. Seated, from left to right, are: Noble Henderson, W. Scatamacchia, Charles Menut, Tom Turner, William Walker, Clarence Whippee, Hugh Nelson, and William McMasters; (standing) Bill Bourdelais, Harry Lewis, Clifford Titcomb, Mr. Sylvester, William O'Donnell, Angus McAskill, Herbert Clark, Ralph Call, Roger Perry, Joseph Pattee, unknown, Lorenzo Hyde, Al Perry, George Harden, Howard Smith, John Saulnier, John A. Pattee, George Spates, unknown, and George Pattee.

Iron and chestnut poles supported the trolley wires and also carried the telephone and signal equipment. Keeping those 50-plus miles of overhead wire and communication devices in top condition kept crews like this one plenty busy.

Linemen were among the highest paid trolley employees, earning as much as 60¢ per hour in 1920, the peak year of wage levels. By 1921, the onslaught of the automobile was affecting ridership severely, forcing the company to cut wages eight to ten percent across the board. By the end of the trolley era in 1929, pays had risen back only to 1920 levels.

There were two carhouses in the division: one on Bridge Street in Pelham (part of which is now St. Patrick's Hall) and, of course, the huge Salem plant. Renovating a car in Salem are, left to right: Harry Haigh, Walter Hunt, Clarence Whippie, Roger Perry, unknown, and Joe Breckles. In 1918, carpenters made about 33¢ per hour, car repairers averaged 28¢, and blacksmiths earned as much as 38¢—or about $3.43 per day. They, too, were victims of the 1921 pay cuts.

James Hadley served both as dispatcher and as an inspector on the Salem Division. Here, he strikes a commanding pose in the office of the Salem carbarn. Keeping track of the cars on the 50-mile system was a formidable task. Missed communications on a Sunday morning in 1903, for example, caused a head-on collision of two open cars on a blind curve near Pelham Center. Six people were killed and more than seventy others were injured, making it the worst trolley accident in New Hampshire history.

Operating the alternating current panel in the Salem substation is William G. Horsch. Power for the system was supplied at 13,200 volts via high tension lines from Portsmouth, supplemented in 1903 by another line from Hampton. The power was converted to the required 600 volts DC in the Salem substation which housed five 300-kilowatt rotary converters, fifteen air-cooled transformers and a 100-kilowatt booster.

These 30-foot Laconia closed cars were fresh from the manufacturer when they were photographed here in the Salem carbarn. Able to accommodate forty passengers, each car was equipped with ten reversible seats and four corner seats, all upholstered in plush. Their interiors were finished in cherry, with ceilings of quartered oak. Because they were used mostly in cold weather, they also boasted electric heaters.

The Salem Division motormen and conductors maintained the highest average running speed in the system. This was due, in part, to the many miles of cross-country right of way they traveled, as well as to the excellent power conditions supplied by the Salem and Pelham substations. Thanks to powerful snowplows like this one, they were able to run uninterrupted through most bad weather and could resume operation quickly after a blizzard.

All Salem Division trolley cars were originally painted carmine red with 24k gold leaf numbers and pin striping. Eight of them even had gold lettering. Starting in 1908, the closed cars were repainted chrome yellow. They had carmine numbers with gold leaf shadows and trim, gray roofs, and green wheel trucks. Open cars were changed to the yellow, burgundy, and green color scheme in 1915. Above, in 1916, is brand new car No. 144, sporting the yellow and carmine motif. Its interior can be seen on p. 2.

Salem Division employees of all categories considered themselves "railroad men" and perceived themselves to be a step above the street railway workers of the Northeastern's other three divisions. Barn and shop workers made certain that the cars were spanking clean inside and out. Motormen and conductors, posed above with dispatcher James Hadley, took great pride in their on-time, accident-free performance.

Although the basic trolley fare was 5¢, you usually couldn't get where you wanted to go for just a nickel. The lines were divided into 5¢ fare zones with two zones between Lawrence and Canobie Lake Park, for example, and two from Haverhill to Canobie. The trip from Haverhill to Lowell passed through five zones, so taking that ride cost a quarter. During the summer, reduced rate round-trip tickets to Canobie were available from all the cities. Discounted commuter rates for "workingmen" were also offered, and students rode for half price. While many other fare and zone structures came and went during the twenty-eight-year era, the actual cost of travel never rose much above original levels.

Extensive timetables were published regularly by the Northeastern. This one, from the summer of 1917, contained advertisements for Canobie Lake Park, as well as for Hampton and Salisbury Beaches—both of which had enjoyed substantial investments by the company in order to attract riders.

To take the family to Salisbury Beach from Salem, you'd first ride thirty-five minutes to Haverhill, then transfer to a Salisbury-bound car. Seventy-five minutes later you'd be basking on the beach! Prior to 1902, getting to Salisbury in less than two hours was unheard of. A Salem to Lawrence trip took a mere thirty-five minutes, with cars leaving twice an hour—even more frequently during busy times.

The bulk of the Salem Division's business came during the summer months when, as today, people came from all over to visit Canobie Lake Park. Waiting to pick up passengers at the Point A interchange are George Woodbury and Walter Hadley, the crew of car No. 90. At the station are some waiting passengers along with Robert H. Dunbar, division superintendent from 1903 to 1907. The porch of Heaps' store can be seen at the extreme right of the photo.

While waiting for your connection at Point A, you could enjoy a Cascade Ginger Ale, a quick lunch, or maybe even a 5¢ Nichols ice cream cone. They all were available at J.B. Heaps' store, right across the tracks from the station. Heaps' was a busy establishment, thanks to its location at the junction of four major trolley lines. Many a passenger spent time on the store's porch benches, provided as free promotional gimmicks by the businesses advertised on them.

Almost there! School children eagerly wait for their trolley, No. 115 bound from Lawrence, to finally reach Canobie Lake Park. The car is waiting here at Point C junction either for connecting cars or for clearance to proceed to the park. Point C was located just a few hundred feet west of North Policy Street and about the same distance north of today's Northeastern Boulevard. It was the intersection of the Lawrence to Canobie and Haverhill to Canobie lines.

We're here! After heading north from Point C, the tracks crossed Brookdale Road at the bottom of the hill just west of North Policy, and entered Canobie Lake Park beneath the sign pictured on the next page. Trolleys exited the park after traveling a large loop that returned them to a southbound direction. Beyond the fountain (above) is the trolley starter's office which sat in the center of the loop.

Two

A Nice Place to Go on Sundays

Canobie Lake Park was an integral part of the street railway investors' original plans and was critical to their success. Serving as a destination reachable for the most part only by trolley, Canobie drew thousands of pleasure riders and charter groups. The Massachusetts Northeastern enjoyed high profits during the months that the park was open each year, then barely scraped by during the winter. Canobie was designed by architect Frank M. Blaisdell and built by the Massachusetts Construction Company. In May of 1902, Warren W. Potter of Haverhill sub-contracted to build the restaurant, boathouse, dancing pavilion, Ping-Pong building, shelters and restrooms—all in two months, at a total cost of $15,500.

Granite State Grove

CANOBIE, LAKE, N. H.

Situated on one of the most charming and picturesque sheets of water in the state is equipped for picnic parties of any size. On the direct line of B. & M. R. R., only 35 miles from Boston. Good ball grounds, skating rink, dance hall, row boats, steamboat, bowling alley, swings, etc. First-class restaurant on the grounds All vegetables fresh from the garden.

Grounds and Restaurant Open Sundays.

For particulars address

O. A. KENEFICK,

Telephone Exchange. **Box 7, Canobie Lake, N. H.**

The choice of the Canobie shore for the trolley company's park was a fairly safe one, as the lake had already been attracting day-trippers for more than half a century. With the coming of the railroad in 1849, an enterprising businessman saw the potential of Policy Pond (Canobie's name at the time) as a recreational destination. In a Windham stand of pines near the corner of North Policy Street and Route 111, just up the hill from the train stop, Policy Pond Grove opened in 1850. At first, people came to rent boats and to fish, but as the grove's popularity grew, other attractions were added. The property sold to Abel Dow in 1877 and, as this turn-of-the-century ad and postcard show, the place eventually boasted every amenity needed to assure a pleasant outing. With its name changed to Granite State Grove, the park continued in operation until 1909, when fire—and a lack of insurance money to rebuild—finally put it out of business.

Known as Haverhill, Polis, and then Policy Pond, the lake got the name Canobie in 1885. In that year a railroad station was built at the Policy Pond stop. Railroad officials chose to name the new station "Canobie" in honor of nearby Windham's Scottish heritage.

Summer cottages had already begun to spring up around the lake by the time of the name change. None, however, were as grand as this one, built in 1895 by Levi Woodbury on North Policy Street, across from today's water treatment plant.

Levi Woodbury was a Salem native who made his money in Washington, D.C., operating the St. James Hotel and a fleet of Potomac steamboats. Most other cottagers on Canobie were business or professional people from Greater Lawrence, many of whom were Roman Catholic. To serve their summer worship needs, the first Roman Catholic church in Salem (above) was built in 1910 at the junction of Canobie Avenue and Lake Shore Road. Called Immaculate Conception, it remained in use for many years.

For those who couldn't afford a whole summer at the lake, trolleys provided the way to have a day's vacation there for just a nickel or a dime. When Canobie Lake Park opened on Saturday, August 23, 1902, streetcars packed to triple their designed capacity arrived at the trolley loop all day. By 1905, when motorman Dan McLean and conductor Tom Butler brought this car around the loop, the park was already a summer tradition for thousands.

The trolley loop, shown here about 1909, was the point of entry and exit for all visitors until after World War I, when some arrangements were reluctantly made for auto entry and parking. Since Canobie was a trolley property, automobiles were discouraged. Some visitors that first day in 1902 definitely wished for another way to get home. That night, too many people and too few trolleys forced some Lawrence residents to walk home, while others rode back in company-hired horse-drawn wagons.

In Canobie's early years America was in the throes of a picture postcard craze. Postcard collecting was all the rage and sending postcards, even across town, was not only a good way to gloat, but also a practical way to communicate—fewer than two percent of Americans had a telephone back then. There were postcards for every taste. This one, with its real felt pennant and risqué sentiment, probably stirred up a little excitement when it was received!

After stepping off the trolley, visitors walked northwest a distance to the "entrance" of the park, marked by these two stone pillars. Today, this original entrance sits well inside the park, near the men's and ladies' cottages at the south end of the dance hall. One of the stone pillars still remains, on the lake side of what is now the kiddie ride area. Yes, the sign in the foreground says "Keep off the Grass!"

This *c.* 1910 color poster of the park, looking south, contains many wonderful details. Starting at the top and moving counter-clockwise, the trolley loop and starter's station are top left, near the carousel. Next is the figure-eight roller coaster, followed by the swing ride, the photography studio, and the giant athletic field. At bottom center sits the bowling alley building, which also housed the House of Mirth fun house and other attractions.

On the lake shore, starting at the right, is the boathouse. To its left is the 600-seat restaurant, followed by the ice cream pavilion and the dance hall. Next come the penny arcade, the men's and ladies' cottages, and finally, the popular Japanese Theater. From there, Lovers Walk curves around the shore to the Canobie Lake Hotel (not pictured). In the center of the park is the electric fountain, a focal point and trademark for nearly a century. Fanning out from it are the some of the beautiful walkways and landscaping for which the 50-acre park was renowned.

The old apple tree with its rustic platform sat just inside the pillared entrance. It was a lovers' haven and shows up on more old postcards than almost any other feature of the park. Canobie's current owners recently planted a new apple tree in the same spot where the original stood, after painstakingly determining its exact location.

The Penny Arcade was just one of the beautiful buildings that helped establish Canobie Lake Park as one of New England's premier resorts. It featured all sorts of coin-operated games and attractions. Many a young man tried to impress his girl by demonstrating his skill on the "Strength Tester" or the "Grip-O-Meter." The roof sign advertising "Automatic Vaudeville" referred to Mutoscopes, crank-operated machines that simulated motion pictures by flipping a series of still photos.

The Circle Swing, part of the original park, was a thrill ride in 1902. Versions of it lasted well into the 1970s, all in the same location near the electric fountain. Shiny rocketships were the last of four eras of seats to be installed on its cables. Charles Ambler was the original concessionaire and operator of Canobie's swing ride. He would come to town each summer and board at the Fairmont House, off South Policy Street, for the months the park was open.

Three shots for a nickel or sixteen for a quarter let you impress your friends at the Shooting Gallery. That 25¢ was quite expensive considering that it was an hour's wage for the average person—but winning a prize for your betrothed made it well worth the sacrifice! Legend has it that the gallery's rifles were not permanently fixed in place until after one angry patron picked one up and shot at another!

A refreshment stand still sits today where this one did in 1909—right across from the entrance to the big roller coaster.

Concessionaires R. E. Graves and Charles J. Ramsdell ran all of Canobie's food service operations for many years—except for vending machines, which the trolley company reserved for itself. Candy and ice cream were made right on the premises.

Graves and Ramsdell, who had previously managed the dining halls at Harvard and hotels on the Isles of Shoals, also handled food service for numerous other trolley parks.

Visiting Canobie for the first time was, for many, as exciting as a first visit to Disney World is today. Admission to the park was free, but there was a charge for most rides and attractions. Box Ball Bowling was one of the first games visitors came upon after getting off the trolley.

Bowling was one of the most popular pastimes at Canobie for several decades, and one of the few sports considered proper enough for women to participate in at the turn of the century. In this photo, however, the women sat primly, watching from the sidelines, as men—straw hats donned and neckties swaying—stood at the foul line and aimed. There were ten lanes at the bowling alley and pins were reset manually by pin boys for a few cents a string.

Canobie pin boys from South Lawrence posed with their bosses for this 1912 photo. From left to right are: (front row) Master Hickey, Ed Retelle, Ed Norton, Al Retelle, Paddy Linehan, and E. Raitte; (back row) Ed Begley, Spatter Pendergast, George Baker, Barty Conelly, Walter Scanlon, Joe Petelle, and Mr. Redmond. Al Retelle became a Lawrence mailman when he grew up. His brother Ed became the city's fire chief.

With its shaded walks, lush landscaping, and cool breezes, Canobie Lake Park was the perfect escape from summer in the city. Visitors loved to watch monkeys frolicking in their cage near the dance hall and deer grazing in a special park out behind the roller coaster.

The trolley company constructed this building to house bowling—and to cash in on the epidemic of "Ping-Pongitis" that was sweeping the country in 1902. Invented in England in the 1890s, Ping-Pong became so popular here that stores couldn't keep nets and paddles in stock. The fad passed quickly. Soon the Ping-Pong area was occupied by a glass-walled maze, forerunner of the fun houses which would locate here later. Here, too, was the Japanese String Game, in which one of hundreds of hanging strings was pulled to win trinkets or beautiful lacquered boxes.

Swimming was still allowed in the lake when the park first opened in 1902. Just a year later, however, Canobie became the town water supply and swimming was prohibited. A 250,000-gallon brick and cement pool, lined with white enamel tile, was added to the park around 1912. Shown above *c.* 1915, it was drained daily and refilled with fresh water pumped in directly from the lake.

Pool patrons could even rent bathing suits if they didn't have one of their own. The expense was well worth it for the chance to dive from the high ladders or just cool off on a hot summer day. For kids, especially, "shooting the chute" was half the fun. Seen above, the chute was a sheet metal slide continually bathed in a film of re-circulating water. Any repairs needed on it were done by trolley company tinsmiths.

The showpiece and pride of the park, even today, is the carousel. Built in the late 1800s and believed to have originally been steam-powered, it became one of Canobie's first rides. Owned by Carl Braun, it was operated as a concession. Like most other concessionaires at the park, Braun paid an annual fee and a percentage of the ride's gross receipts to the trolley company. The carousel's original music-making device was replaced sometime in the '20s or '30s by the beautiful 1917 Wurlitzer military band organ seen here. It plays bass and snare drums, metal chimes, and, of course, the organ—all automatically. Now running on punched paper rolls like a player piano, the Wurlitzer's music was originally coded onto punched cardboard sheets, fan folded much like today's computer paper.

The 2,854-seat Japanese Theater (above) was one of the park's most stunning features during the trolley years. An advertising brochure from 1903 describes "acres of seats shot through by the trunks of forest monarchs," and an immense colored awning stretching over the seating area to block the sun's rays. Admission was 10¢ or 20¢, depending on seat location, for the theater's band concerts, vaudeville shows, and musical comedies. In 1913, motion pictures were shown but proved to be a flop. Vaudeville returned for a few more years and movies were later re-introduced—successfully—as well. Since the sides of the theater were open, large canvas tarps were rolled down to darken it for movie projection. The audience photo below was taken *c.* 1909. The little girl third from the left in the front row is Grace McMasters, a long-time resident of Salem.

King the Diving Horse, shown here on a stock publicity postcard, appeared at the park in August of 1907—part of a traveling act handled by J. W. Gorman. High-diving horses were very popular at the turn of the century, regularly taking the plunge at large amusement parks like Coney Island and Revere Beach.

King was not the only aquatic star to perform at Canobie in the early days. Human high-divers were also featured, in diving exhibitions from a 60-foot platform at the swimming pool. And Ethelda Bleibtrey—a three-medal winner in Antwerp for the first U.S. women's Olympic swim team in 1920—put on shows at the pool all one summer.

Canobie was designed with this electric fountain as its centerpiece. All major park walkways ultimately led to it, and more visitors have probably had their pictures taken in front of it than in front of any other structure at the park. Illuminated on most summer nights since 1902, the fountain has served as a romantic backdrop for generations of courting young lovers.

There were two restaurants on the grounds, both operated by Graves & Ramsdell. One was a lunch counter which sat about a dozen people and also served as a souvenir store, and the other was the much larger main restaurant shown in these photos. Designed to seat 600 people, the building was constructed in the shape of a St. George's Cross. That way, all rows of tables were near windows, allowing every diner to enjoy lake breezes. A fire eventually destroyed the structure and another was built in its place. A third, quite modern cafeteria-style restaurant, replaced that one on the same spot in the early 1980s. Food service today is handled by the Marriott Corporation.

Modern roller coasters made their first appearance at Coney Island in 1884, offering thrills and terror that immediately made them an amusement park must. Canobie opened with this figure-eight coaster in 1902, operated by concessionaire D. F. Bowser. He later went on to become park superintendent for twenty-one years.

Roller coaster passengers boarded through the entrance shown above, *c.* 1909. The figure-eight was replaced sometime between 1914 and 1924 with a "double-dip" coaster in the same spot. The giant wooden structure that stands today was installed in 1936. Roller coasters have remained so popular through the years that, by the 1990s, Canobie had three to choose from.

Canobie Lake itself, of course, was a major park attraction. Thousands enjoyed many an afternoon on the lake in rental canoes, rowboats, and fishing skiffs. Operated by Graves & Ramsdell, the boathouse concession boasted forty-two rowboats and twenty-four canoes by 1913. In later years, as boats wore out and were not replaced, the boathouse was used as a storage building. It has now been resurrected by the park's current owners for use as an arcade.

Visitors from the very beginning enjoyed lake cruises on the park's powered excursion boats. The queen of the small fleet was the *Mineola*, pictured above in 1909. It made regular half-hour trips around the lake for a fare of 10¢. Later renamed the *Martha Washington*, the boat served delighted passengers for more than thirty years. Smaller launches were rented to private parties. Around 1904 there was even a steam launch, operated by Robert J. Adams of Lawrence, to shuttle cottagers back and forth from the park to their camps on the lake.

People donned their best clothes and showiest hats for a visit to Canobie in the early decades. From the time it first opened, the park promoted itself as a wholesome family resort. Trolley company officials were very sensitive to the fact that many amusement parks were gaining seedy reputations. Even Coney Island, the granddaddy of them all, was being referred to as "Sodom by the Sea." All of Canobie's owners have gone to great lengths to maintain a positive atmosphere—one of the major reasons for the park's longevity. A tree-lined path known as Lovers' Walk (above) meandered south along the shore, stretching from the park's south grove to the Canobie Lake Hotel. The hotel (below) was located at the sharp curve on today's Canobie Avenue, straight in from Brookdale Road.

Built by Lawrence Alderman Paul Hannagan in the early 1900s, the Canobie Lake Hotel had thirty rooms and a two-story porch from which guests could enjoy lake views. The establishment was sold to James A. Sayer about 1922 and continued in operation until the early 1930s. During Sayer's ownership, band leader Paul Whiteman visited the hotel, as did Indy race car drivers and Olympic champions. One winter, a toboggan slide was constructed, extending from the hotel's roof to the lake. An outdoor ice rink also existed at one time, serving as the practice spot for the Woodbury High hockey team in 1929. The property included an ice house, seen below at right. Ice was cut on Canobie by Frank Lundberg's Salem Ice Company, then stored here to serve the summer needs of cottages and the hotel.

Ever seen one of these? It's a *c.* 1912 "moon shot" taken at Canobie's photo studio—and almost every old family album in the Merrimack Valley contains at least one.

Americans were having a love affair with the moon in the early twentieth century, thanks to the Trip to the Moon adventure ride that mesmerized millions at Buffalo's Pan-American Exposition in 1901. The first special effects amusement ride ever, it was tame by today's standards. But back in 1901 it was enough to get the whole nation talking—and singing. Before long, "By the Light of the Silvery Moon" and "Shine On, Harvest Moon" were hit songs, and people like the Jennings family of Salem were lining up to pose for celestial photos like this one.

The photo studio was one of the park's original attractions and, in the days before everyone owned a Kodak Brownie, it was a busy place indeed. Posing for a photograph back then was no easy task. It required the right clothes, the right "this is for posterity" stance, and the ability to remain motionless while the photographer performed his magic.

The Sayer family had this now-faded portrait taken at the studio in about 1916. Like most photos taken there, it was printed as a postcard, ready to mail to friends not lucky enough to be at the park. The Sayers, however, didn't need to mail theirs; they were at Canobie most of the time.

James A. Sayer, standing with his wife Anne, was a concessionaire for many years. From 1912 through 1929 he operated the swimming pool, theater, and pool room. Later, he brought Skee Ball to the park and ran other attractions as well. Little James A. Sayer Jr., seated with his grandfather (and dog Teddy), grew up to become a Salem lawyer and judge—but not before he built the still-popular Canobie fish pond.

At some unrecorded date in time, the Canobie Lake Studio ceased operations, possibly "snapped" out of fashion by the Kodak Brownie. By the 1940s, the building was serving as Canobie's first-aid "emergency room." Today the structure survives, empty and unused, in among the twists and turns of the Tin Lizzy Auto ride.

One of the most-used facilities at the park was the giant athletic field (seen in its entirety on p. 30). It was completely fenced in and contained a running track, a ball field, two grandstands, and a pavilion used by outing groups. In the *c.* 1907 postcard above, crowds are leaving the field after a baseball game.

Sunday school and church picnics, club, lodge, and factory outings were all aggressively pursued by park management. Chartered trolleys brought hundreds of thousands of people to Canobie over the years to party, play, and picnic in the athletic field. The happy group above was photographed on a company outing in 1908.

The first big outing at Canobie was held on Labor Day 1902, when almost 10,000 members, family, and friends of the Haverhill Central Labor Union converged on the park. A large ox was killed and roasted for the occasion. Special events took place all day, including a Gaelic football game in the morning and running races in the afternoon. The running track was 2/10 of a mile in length, illuminated for night events by arc lamps mounted on standards bordering the oval. The tall pole in the bottom photo had notched steps for climbing races; another one like it stood nearby. The outing pavilion and the park's water tank are seen in both of these photographs, taken about 1909. Both structures were destroyed in the hurricane of 1938.

Time to go home. For two decades almost everyone left Canobie by trolley, from this open station where boarding areas were marked for Haverhill, Lawrence, Lowell, and Nashua. By the beginning of the 1920s, however, the trolley company was wrestling with the onslaught of the automobile. More and more people were opting to drive their own vehicles to Canobie rather than taking streetcars to the park. Large numbers of "party trucks" also began arriving, their stake-sided open backs carrying loads of passengers up from Boston.

Trying to protect trolley revenues, the company attempted to discourage motor vehicles with a parking fee and limited parking space—giving birth to a local cottage industry in the process. If Canobie was unwilling to accommodate drivers, neighboring landowners like Lavington Dyson certainly were not. Dyson's property sat directly across North Policy Street from today's park entrance. Spotting an opportunity, he promptly turned his yard into a parking lot for party trucks, parking as many as a hundred every Sunday—at a dollar apiece.

MASSACHUSETTS NORTHEASTERN STREET RAILWAY COMPANY

NOTICE OF DISCONTINUANCE.

NOTICE IS HEREBY GIVEN THAT AT 12.30 A. M. ON SUNDAY, MARCH 17, 1929, the street railway service now furnished by this company's car line operated between Hampshire Road, Methuen, Massachusetts, near the Methuen, Massachusetts - Salem, New Hampshire, boundary line and the Methuen, Massachusetts-Haverhill, Massachusetts, boundary line near Ayer's Village, Massachusetts, including the operation of all of this company's main line, sidings and railway system lying within the limits of the town of Salem, New Hampshire, WILL BE PERMANENTLY DISCONTINUED.

Massachusetts Northeastern Street Railway Company,

By C. L. Bartlett,

Vice-President.

March 1, 1929.

The 1920s were difficult years for the Mass. Northeastern. Business was collapsing under the weight of the tiny automobile. By 1923, the company was before the New Hampshire Public Service Commission, requesting to abandon lines to Pelham, Dracut, and Nashua. There were now automobiles in the driveways of all but eight homes served by the Pelham line, and daily trolley revenues for two weeks in January had averaged only $24.87. Wages, maintenance, and schedules were cut back on all the lines as ridership continued to drop. At the same time, management was raising fares in a desperate attempt to stay in business. It was a vicious cycle that angered the public and hastened the company's demise. The town of Salem declined to act on an option to help keep the Salem lines in operation—and on Sunday, March 17, 1929, the last electric car rolled out of town.

Receiver's Sale at Auction

Monday, November 30 and
Tuesday, December 1, 1931

All the Right, Title and Interest

OF THE

Massachusetts Northeastern Street Railway Company

in and to

each of the following properties

CANOBIE LAKE PARK, Salem, New Hampshire
CAR HOUSE, Salem, New Hampshire
CAR HOUSE, Plaistow, New Hampshire
CAR HOUSE, Amesbury, Massachusetts
CAR HOUSE, Newburyport, Massachusetts
RECREATION GROVE, Salisbury, Massachusetts
OLD POWER HOUSE LOTS, Newburyport, Massachusetts
OLD CAR HOUSE (SCHOOL STREET) LOT, Merrimac, Massachusetts
MARSH LAND, Plum Island, Massachusetts

Sale subject to confirmation by the Court

Canobie went out of business at the end of the 1929 season. An attempt to auction it off in September failed when the reported top bid of $26,200 was not accepted. The trolley company was forced into bankruptcy in January of 1930, and its properties were finally sold the next year. The cover of the auction catalogue appears above. The Canobie auction took place on the walkway between the swimming pool and the carousel, with several hopeful bidders in attendance. One was Lawrence businessman Louis Pearl, who reportedly dropped out when bids reached $15,000. The gavel came down at $17,000 plus taxes—less than one-twelfth of what the park had been valued at in 1925. Patrick J. Holland of Lawrence now owned Canobie Lake Park and a new era would soon begin.

Three
The Holland Years

It took Pat Holland only eight weeks in the spring of 1932 to get the park back in shape and ready to reopen. Hundreds of men went to work trimming overgrown trees and shrubs, repairing buildings and attractions, and giving everything a fresh coat of paint. One of the first things to be remedied was the nagging parking situation. With the trolleys gone, the park's main entrance was now on North Policy Street. Holland gave the job of constructing the main gate (above) to Carl Olson & Sons of Lawrence and, at the same time, began work on a parking lot to hold 5,000 cars—all of which would park for free.

How was it that Pat Holland could come up with the money necessary to save and improve Canobie during the depression? Generations of park-goers have this concrete-paving machine to thank. With it, he had completed two million dollars worth of road-building contracts between 1925 and 1931, constructing over a hundred miles of concrete highways in New Hampshire, Massachusetts, and Vermont. Holland began his career about 1911, working with his brother Philip in Lawrence. After moving to Colorado and sustaining severe leg injuries in a train accident, he returned to Lawrence with his wife, Catherine, and young son, Maurice. Small cement-laying projects soon led to major contracts. Holland was on his way.

One of the factors that had made Canobie unattractive to potential buyers was the large additional investment it would take to update the park's electrical system. The entire place operated on 600 volts of direct current, just as the trolley cars had. Holland spent a great deal of money rewiring everything to handle the modern 110 and 220 volt alternating current.

By the time of Canobie's grand reopening on Memorial Day weekend in 1932, one of the few reminders of the park's origin was this old streetcar. Holland had placed it in the picnic grove as a testimonial to the electric railway that created Canobie. Mrs. Holland came up with a testimonial of her own, composing a poem that would become the park's theme song. It was set to music and played at the dance hall on opening night by Mickie Alpert and his Smiling Admirals, the Boston band engaged for the festivities.

Visitors on opening day found many of the same attractions that had delighted them in earlier years, but some park concessionaires weren't able to get the deals they wanted. The carousel was dismantled and stored in a barn on Pond Street for two years while its future was in limbo. Holland wanted to buy the ride and reportedly offered the Brauns $500. Knowing it was worth much more, they refused. Only after a futile search for a similar carousel did Holland finally raise his offer by several thousand. The Brauns then accepted and the merry-go-round became a permanent fixture at Canobie.

The carousel's hand-carving represents the work of three different firms: Looff, Dentzel, and Stein & Goldstein. An outer ring of animals was added to the ride in the 1920s, bringing the total of hand-carved horses to forty-six. The Wurlitzer military band organ (pictured on p. 38) still provides music for the merry-go-round today. A side view of the mechanical wizard, taken in the 1950s, is shown at left.

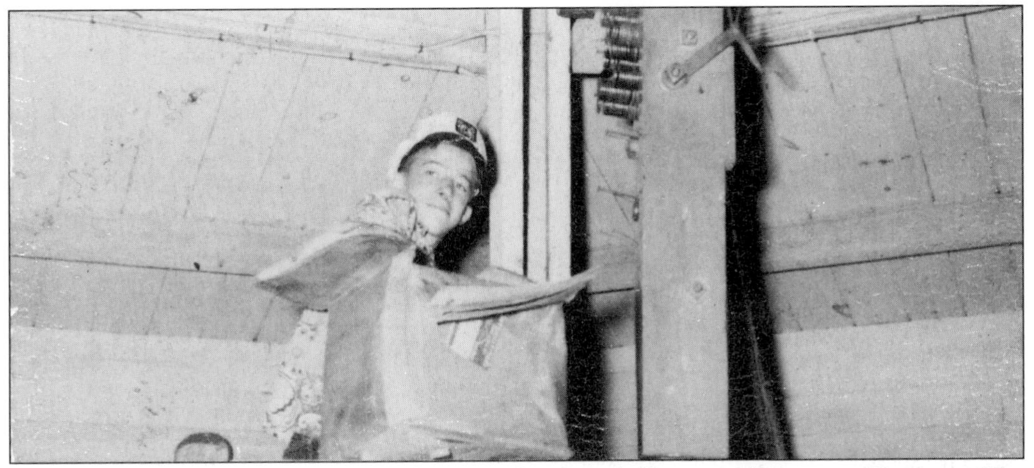

"Grab the brass ring and win a free ride" was a familiar challenge at the carousel for years. The rings were dispensed from a steel arm just within reach of riders on the eighteen outer horses. Stretching for a ring on each pass, riders tossed losers—plain steel rings—into a basket, then tried again for a brass one on the next revolution. Since the dispensing arm held only thirty-six rings, it required constant refilling during each ride. Fifteen-year-old Salemite Lester Hall was photographed in the 1950s (above) with a supply of rings ready to be fed into the arm. The rings were featured on Thursday through Sunday nights through 1957. The next year they were discontinued all together due to liability concerns. Hall, who would work at the park for thirty years, was given the honor of loading the rings for the very last time (below).

No trip to Canobie was complete without a stop at the curvy, trick mirrors. It was simple fun that none of us could resist. Tall, short, fat, thin—you could even get your head or legs to separate from your body if you did it just right! At left, Daniel Donabedian, of Salem, tried out a new look in 1938.

Who needed a Charles Atlas course when this mirror could turn you into a broad-shouldered Adonis?

The mirrors were a feature in Canobie's first fun house, the House of Mirth. They were later moved and mounted on the outside of the swimming pool building so that a whole row of them greeted you, on your left, as you first entered the park.

The swimming tank, as the pool was called in early 1930s ads, was one of the largest open-air pools in the area. Pat Holland spruced it up with new spring boards and a new diving ladder. In 1934 the New England Championship Swimming Meet was held here. The attraction is still in operation today, although a brand new pool replaced the original in the late 1970s.

In 1936, a giant modern roller coaster replaced the old double-dip model. Named The Greyhound, the thrilling new ride was so much the pride of the park that this new entrance was built especially for it. Manufactured by the Philadelphia Toboggan Company in 1930, the coaster was purchased by Holland from Lakeview Park in Waterbury, Connecticut. It was shipped to Salem by train and reassembled by Guy Ackerman, a well-known Salem contractor.

Until 1977, the coaster's heavy, careening cars were brought to a stop manually. The operator leaned on a huge lever that actually lifted the cars off the tracks, making them skid to a stop. The roller coaster has been meticulously maintained during its sixty years at Canobie, with someone walking the tracks daily to inspect its condition. In 1954, this 60-foot first hill had to be rebuilt after it was knocked over by a large tree during Hurricane Carol.

A generation or more rode the big coaster for just a dime, handing their coins directly to an attendant. The investment brought forty-five seconds of spine-tingling thrills. Admission to all rides eventually changed to a ticket system, making coin changers like the one on this operator's belt a thing of the past.

Many remember the sign that boasted the coaster's 3,000-foot length as "The Longest Ride In New England." It's shown here on the Greyhound's parking lot curve in the 1930s. The huge parking lot itself was also advertised back then—as the largest one in New Hampshire, with enough spaces to accommodate an unlimited number of "machines."

Here are two views of the same area of the park taken roughly two decades apart. The 1940s photograph above shows the Rumpus, a ride-through fun house which had been called the Pretzel when it first opened at Canobie in 1932. By the time the lower photo was taken, the attraction had been revamped and was again using its original name. The ride went through yet another name change—to The Swamp—before finally being removed in the 1980s. The area to the right of the arcade stretched to the Dodgem building. In the 1940s, the space contained side games such as Pitch 'Til You Win. By the late 1950s, the Roundup (below) was located there. Today, the arcade has expanded into much of the space.

This building (seen in 1909 on p. 38) housed bowling alleys in the back and a fun house in the front when Holland bought the park. He continued its tradition. The alleys were renovated in 1934 and the old fun house was updated. Called Laugh Valley, it is seen above as it appeared in the 1940s.

Laugh Valley was billed as the home of "laugh-a-minute stunts." A trip through ended with the "slide home." Visitors sat on a leather couch that unexpectedly dropped out from under them, dumping them onto this carpeted conveyor-belt. Bowling lasted until the late 1950s and the fun house section was again updated, this time with a spook house theme. Today the fun house and bowling alleys are gone and the building contains, among other things, Canobie's gift shop and Fascination games.

Always an ego booster (or buster), the Rifle Range, as it was called in the Holland years, was an eternally popular spot with the guys. Shooting the real .22 caliber rifles was an exciting event for many. Remember the sharp crack of the shots and the loud clang of the hit targets? Today, the rifles shoot beams of light and elaborate electronic targets respond accordingly.

Another good place to impress your gal or compete with your friends was at the Baseball Game. Budding hurlers took their best shot, pitching balls at a dummy batter and catcher.

A giant cigar, a funny hat—maybe an Indian beaded belt with "Canobie Lake Park" spelled out on it . . . All were fun to consider at the gift shop, but when it came to actually buying, nothing was ever more popular than the kewpie doll. Six inches tall and attached to a bamboo cane, the feather-bedecked kewpie put all three of Frank McHugh's kids through college. McHugh began running the gift shop concession in 1942; his daughter Suzanne still operates it today.

Packed with coin operated games—some new, some old, some ancient—the arcade had something for everyone. Who didn't invest a nickel, at least once, trying for the wristwatch wrapped around a pack of Lucky Strikes in the Rotary Merchandiser? We all stamped messages onto little metal disks, tried the love and strength meters, had our fortunes told by the mechanical old woman in the glass case—and, of course, played a little pinball.

During the Holland years it was the Soda Fountain. Later, this building became the Duck Pond, where dozens of little plastic ducks floated by. You'd pluck one from the water and receive whatever prize corresponded to the number on the duck's bottom. Unfortunately, it was more often the wicker Chinese finger trap rather than the giant stuffed panda bear!

In the relentless quest to score nine perfect fifties, park-goers happily dropped their nickels and pulled the levers on the Skee Ball games. The sound of those nine little brown balls clattering their way down the chute is eternally etched in our memories. It seems there were as many different techniques to rolling the balls as there were players! If the machines were all busy, 25¢ would get you a strip of four photos in the booth on the right.

At the Fish Pond, we tried our luck with rod and reel and, hoping for a high number, always came up with a prize. The fish pond was built by James A. Sayer Jr. of Salem. In 1932 he bought an iron tank in Chelsea, put a turntable into it, added some parts from a Model-T Ford and *voilà,* a new Canobie favorite was born.

One of the all-time great rides at the park—and possibly the most fondly remembered—was the Whip. Located between the merry-go-round and the Dodgems, the ride thundered and screeched, thrilling riders and drowning out the quaint carousel music coming from next door. After almost sixty years of service, the Whip had become difficult to maintain and was retired in the early 1980s.

The Circle Swing, one of Canobie's three original moving rides, brought shouts of glee from countless riders. During its seven decades, the attraction was updated with different sets of seats and a new tower, but it always stood in the same location, just east of the electric fountain. The 1902 swing seats were replaced by biplanes in the 1920s. By the time of this 1930s photograph, military planes hung from the ride's cables.

Whizzing around, just clearing the nearby trees, the ride could put your heart in your throat as it looked, for sure, like you would clip the roof of the popcorn stand as you picked up speed and swung out further and higher. The loose cables seen here indicate that this 1940s photo was taken during the installation of massive new rocketships that would replace the military planes.

The Rocketships were particularly dear to one of the authors, since he ran the ride, for 95¢ an hour, during the entire summer of 1967.

The building at the base housed a huge electric motor and a system of giant, open and unprotected gears—so large that half their diameter was below ground level. The speed controller, with its large, brass, rolling pin-type handle, had been removed and adapted from a trolley car.

Here in full flight, the shiny rocketships just clear the popcorn stand at the lower left. The little building in the center of the photo was home to Miss Kaye, a colorful hand-writing analyst who reportedly always kept a billy club nearby! The fountain and boathouse are in the background.

A *c.* 1940 promotional brochure had this to say about architecture at the park: "Modernistic buildings house the amusements. Bright and wholesome places, freshly painted and well constructed make them safe and inviting." Here, the Dodgem building speaks of its era.

Built by the Dodgem Company of Woodland Street in Lawrence, the bumper cars have always enjoyed long lines of eager drivers awaiting their turns to race—and crash into—each other. Remember the shiny metal floor and the way the overhead hooks sparked with a snap? New cars were purchased from Italy in the early 1970s and a rule requiring one-way traffic was put into effect at roughly the same time.

How do you back this confounded thing up? Popular comedian Jerry Colonna, above at right, hammed it up in this publicity photo, taken during a visit to Canobie on August 2, 1949.

This is the way the Dodgem building looked on September 21, 1938, in the aftermath of one of the most ferocious hurricanes to roar through New England in the twentieth century. Trees and buildings all over the park were damaged or destroyed, resulting in a clean-up effort that took months.

The trolley starter's office, in the center of the loop, became home to the Canobie Lake Park offices during the Holland years. It remained in use for that purpose until 1974, when the park's burgeoning administrative needs could no longer be contained in such a tiny building. After seventy-two years of service, the starter's building was finally retired and new offices were constructed near the roller coaster, behind the big arcade.

The day after the last trolley ran its route, the Massachusetts Northeastern began bus service around the Merrimack Valley. Even the B&M Railroad tried busses to counteract its own war with the automobile. When Canobie reopened in 1931, the former trolley entrance off Brookdale Road became known as Bus Road, a name it still retains today. Mason's Coach Service ran nine times a day between Lawrence and the park that year, picking up and discharging passengers at the former trolley loop, shown here lined with Hudson busses some years later.

Pat Holland died in 1943, leaving his wife Catherine and son Maurice in charge of Canobie Lake Park, which they would continue to operate for fourteen more years. Maurice and his wife, the former Mary K. Sullivan of Salem, were photographed at this Boston Braves game in the late 1940s. Always interested in sports and politics, Maurice brought many professional ball players and prominent politicians to Canobie over the years.

The area between the Dodgems and the penny arcade (also seen on p. 62) has held a multitude of attractions. The fish pond was here at one time, as was a small Ferris wheel. In this photograph, taken before the Roundup was installed in the late 1950s, kiddie rides filled the space. Do you remember this little Austin Healey fire truck? The ladder section had two long rows of seats facing sideways in which visitors could ride from one end of the park to the other.

Though the 1932 stone pillars still stand today, the sign has changed four times. The beautiful arches shown on p. 53 were replaced by this sign in the 1940s. It stood guard over the gates until the early 1960s. Two more versions have been installed since then. The heavy wooden gates have also been replaced, but thanks to the current owners' commitment to Canobie's history and tradition, the new gates are of very similar design.

This "ultra-modern" diesel-type miniature train was installed in 1948. Its route circled the Tom Thumb Miniature Golf Course, passed behind the Dodgems and the Whip, and ran along the parking lot. Today, the miniature golf course area is a parking lot for the park's offices and employees.

Loud and fast, this mahogany Chris Craft speedboat joined Canobie's fleet during the Holland years. On it, passengers were treated to a thrilling tour of the lake shore. In 1949, however, the boat capsized after crossing its own wake in a high-speed turn, killing one adult and one child. The boat was towed back after the incident and returned to service for several more years.

For the less adventurous, the *Ellen C.*, a converted shrimp boat, was available. It took passengers on a comfortable scenic cruise around Canobie Lake. The *Ellen C.* replaced the old *Mineola/Martha Washington* which had served the park so well since the first decade of the century.

Every kid's dream of driving a car came true behind the wheel of one of these. The Custer Cars, as they were known, were miniature gasoline-powered vehicles. In this *c.* 1940 photo, a young lady pulls hers to a stop after a drive around the wooden track.

There was nothing like the breeze in your face, the beat of the organ music, or even taking a break for a hot dog and a Coke. It was all part of the Skating Rink experience. The brave ones practiced jumps in the center while the graceful followed figure-eights painted on the floor. Most of us, though, just tried to stay on our feet—and maybe catch the eye of someone interesting! Canobie had a roller rink from 1902 until the 1970s. This was the last one, built in the 1930s on the former theater site. Today it is used for storage.

Four
The Dance Hall

Of all the attractions at Canobie, the one that holds the fondest memories for many is the ballroom. Whether you two-stepped, jitterbugged, or ponied your way through your younger years, chances are you did it here. The ballroom was a magical place full of excitement and possibilities. It was here that music on the radio came to life every weekend, as it did on this evening in the late 1940s when Freddy Martin appeared. And it was here, on hot summer nights for more than sixty years, that people came from miles around to meet, dance, and fall in love.

The dancing pavilion, as it was called, opened in 1902. It was operated during the trolley years by the Carl Braun family, who also ran Roseland in Methuen and the Commodore Ballroom in Lowell. During the early years the hall was illuminated with dozens of arc lights and incandescents, and the dance floor was surrounded by benches on which spectators sat to watch dancers glide by. Afternoon "tea dances" were popular back then, and singers used megaphones to be heard.

When Pat Holland bought the park, he moved the stage to the north end of the dance hall, added a soda fountain to the south end, installed a modern sound system and a verandah, and updated the decor. This is the way the renovated interior looked on a crowded night in the early 1930s.

Canobie's "official" orchestra in the early 1930s was that of Jean Ippolito, known to thousands in the Northeast as Val Jean. The Lawrence, Massachusetts, saxophonist attended the New England Conservatory of Music and organized his own orchestra, Val Jean and his Arcadians, in 1927. The group traveled the East, giving many prominent local musicians their start. When Pat Holland reopened the park in 1932, the band was featured regularly, now under a new name: Val Jean and his Canobie Lake Orchestra. Live radio shows on NBC's Blue network were broadcast from the dance hall for a time and Val Jean's music wafted over the airwaves far and wide, adding to his popularity.

Val Jean was not the only area orchestra to draw crowds to Canobie over the years. Roland Russell, Frankie Kahn, Tony Brown, and Ted Herbert were also popular names on the marquee during the '30s, '40s and early '50s. Russell, like most local music men, held a regular day job and devoted nights and weekends to performing. The Lawrence native and his orchestra made memories for thousands with their dreamy waltzes and nightly sign-off song, "I'll See You In My Dreams."

From the mid-1920s until the early 1940s, check dancing was the rage. Men purchased tickets (usually 10¢ each, or three for a quarter), asked a lady to dance, then handed one ticket to a collector before entering the dance floor. After the band finished a short set, another ticket had to be used to dance again. By the time this photo was taken in the late '40s, paying by the dance had long-been replaced by "free dancing," with one admission charged to both men and women for the whole evening.

Because Canobie's ballroom was never air-conditioned, dancers really worked up a thirst on hot summer evenings. The refreshment area, added to the dance hall in 1932, quickly became a popular spot. Perhaps its busiest night ever occurred on August 3, 1942. Glenn Miller made his last appearance at Canobie that evening, on a farewell tour of New England before joining the Air Force. (Miller's plane mysteriously disappeared over the English Channel two years later.) The crowd swelled to almost 5,500 that night and refreshment sales boomed. Attendants sold every bit of soda they could find, including all the dusty old display bottles that had been stacked up on the counter for years.

During the 1930s, the country's most popular big bands began rolling into Canobie at a dizzying pace that would continue for more than fifteen years. For an admission price of less than a dollar, mill operatives from Lawrence, farm kids from Salem, and shoe workers from Haverhill found a common denominator at Canobie—the hottest music of the moment, performed live and in person. Small newspaper ads on Thursday nights and posters like the one at left were all it took to draw thousands. On many Friday evenings the population of the ballroom was twice that of the entire town of Salem.

While the big bands were featured most often, the solo performers they spawned also drew sizable crowds on their own. Jerry Colonna, shown below in 1949, was paid $2,000 to appear for the weekend. Once a saxophonist with Jimmy Dorsey and Woody Herman, Colonna soared to national popularity as a comedian after his antics on stage led to a recording that was named the funniest of 1938.

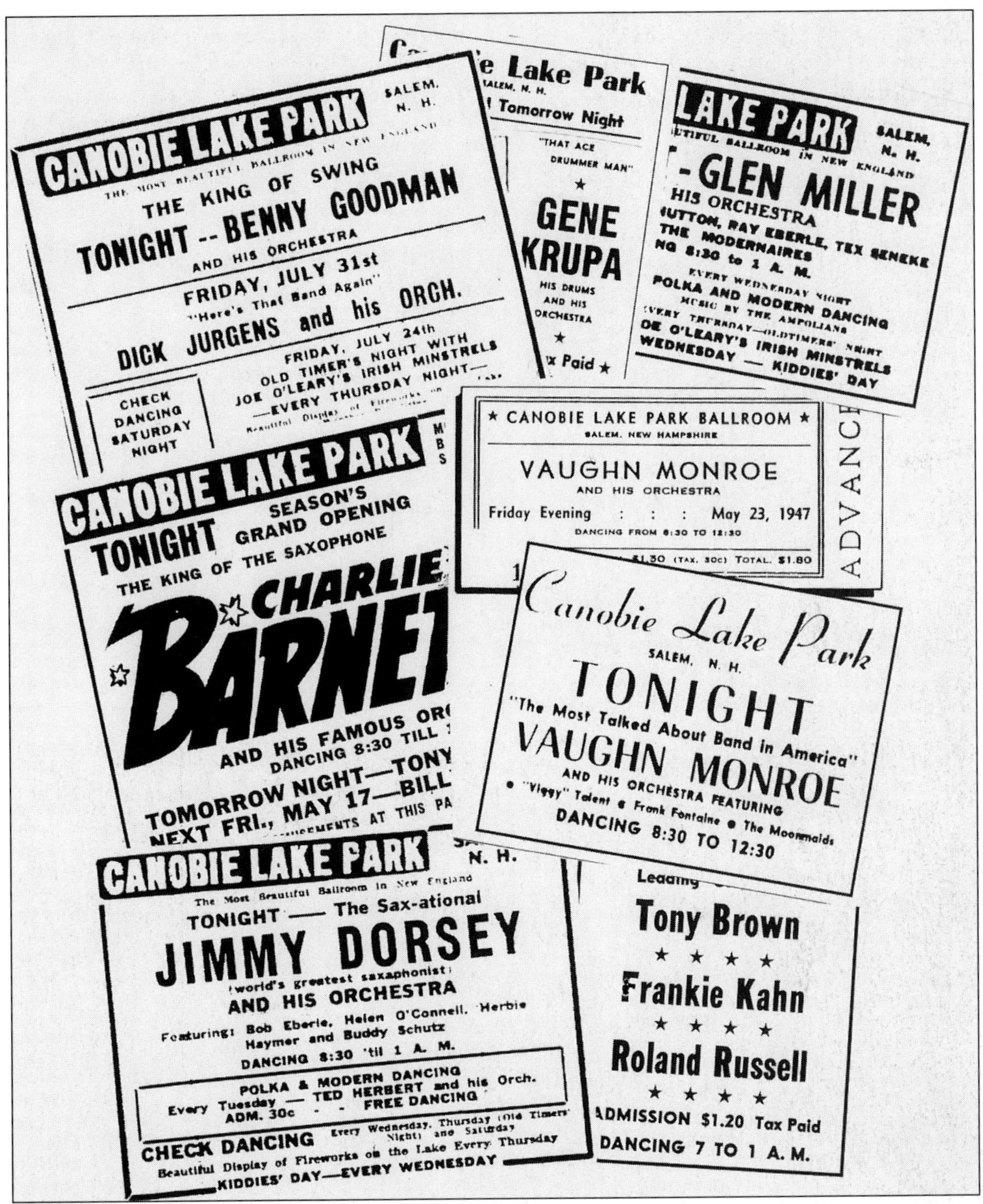

Newspaper ads from the ballroom's heyday read like a *Who's Who* of the big band era: Duke Ellington, Guy Lombardo, Harry James, Count Basie, Woody Herman, Louis Armstrong, Horace Heidt, Charlie Spivak, Stan Kenton . . .. The seemingly endless string of one-nighters usually went off without a hitch. Occasionally, however, an anxious crowd was disappointed—an orchestra showed up too late to play or, in the case of one Louis Prima date, the band arrived but the instruments didn't.

Tommy Dorsey appeared at Canobie a number of times. Pictured above on stage in the 1940s, and below backstage with Maurice Holland, Dorsey was known as "The Sentimental Gentleman of Swing." His orchestra was hailed as the greatest all-around dance band of them all. Tommy mesmerized audiences with his trombone playing, as well as with the talents of his sidemen. Bunny Berigan, Buddy Rich, and Nelson Riddle were among the musicians who played with the band over the years. Singers Jack Leonard, Frank Sinatra, Jo Stafford, the Pied Pipers, and Connie Haines brought Dorsey huge hits, including "Marie," "Embraceable You," and "I'll Never Smile Again."

Jimmy Dorsey (above, on sax) formed the Dorsey Brothers Orchestra with Tommy in 1934. They went their separate ways just a year later, however, when a blow-up between them caused Tommy to walk off a New York stage and out of the band for good. For the next eighteen years the brothers performed separately, often following each other on the summer dance hall circuit. In 1940, for example, Jimmy appeared at Canobie on August 2; Tommy played there three weeks later.

"Swing and Sway with Sammy Kaye" was a familiar slogan during the big band era. With hits like "Harbor Lights" and "It Isn't Fair," Kaye's orchestra set ideal tempos for dancing. And Kaye (standing) fronted the band with style and grace. Critics knocked his music as "mickey-mouse;" mechanical and lacking depth. Fans, on the other hand, loved it—especially novelty routines like "So You Want to Lead a Band" that allowed audience members to become part of the show.

With the outbreak of World War II came gas rationing, tire shortages, a twenty percent federal amusement tax, and a scarcity of dance partners for young women. Musicians, too, became scarce, as they entered the service in droves. Rumors flew about the fate of Canobie and its ballroom. Park owners had to run ads in the early summer of 1942 assuring patrons that the season would go on as usual.

For some bands, the war brought great success. Les Brown, for example, played from military camps across the country on Coca-Cola's *Spotlight* radio show, and had his greatest hit ever, "Sentimental Journey," with Doris Day.

The end of the war in 1945 brought celebrations and romantic reunions. It also brought big crowds to Canobie to hear favorite bands like Harry James, whose Kitty Kallen hit, "It's Been a Long, Long Time," would top the charts that autumn. New bands were emerging as well, some as a direct result of wartime tragedies. Tex Beneke (above), a long-time featured saxophonist with Glenn Miller, took over that band for a short while after the war, then went out on his own.

When he played Canobie in 1947, Beneke (above, at center) attracted almost 4,000 to the ballroom. Big bands had always featured vocalists and Canobie patrons had heard the best: Peggy Lee with Benny Goodman; Sarah Vaughan with Earl Hines; and Frank Sinatra with Tommy Dorsey. Record-buying teenagers, especially, loved the singers. As a result, it wasn't long until many vocalists became more popular than the bands they sang for—and began making record deals on their own.

Although big bands continued to draw good crowds for a few years after the war, more changes were in the air. Returning servicemen were marrying, buying homes, and starting families. And just as the focus shifted from going out to staying home, television came along to provide a convenient new form of entertainment. A Canobie ad for Gene Krupa in 1948 ironically foreshadowed the changes to come: everyone attending that night would be eligible to win a fabulous door prize—a free TV set.

Another new band to emerge after the war was Ralph Flanagan's. A one-time pianist for Sammy Kaye and a long-time arranger for many orchestras, the handsome Flanagan had never set his sights on becoming a band leader. Through a fluke and a promoter's desire to cash in on Glenn Miller's lingering popularity, however, that's exactly what he became.

Flanagan was one of several, including Beneke, to gain money and fame from the Miller sound. But unlike Beneke, Flanagan had never even played with Glenn Miller. The only thing they had in common, in fact, was the same sponsor, Chesterfield cigarettes.

When Flanagan played Canobie in 1950, more than 3,800 clamoring fans were there to greet him. It was one of the last times so many would turn out to hear a big band. By 1952, attendance had dropped dramatically. Stan Kenton, the biggest draw of the entire season, only brought in 1,800 people. Singers were being booked more and more often. Tony Bennett, Mel Torme, Al Martino, Patti Page—these were the performers people wanted to see. The big band era was over.

It was another ten years before a whole new generation packed the ballroom to hear bands every week. But this time it was rock and roll, not swing music, they lined up to hear. The pied piper of this rejuvenation was one of the nation's first female record producers, Ruth Clennott, who also produced WBZ's *Community Auditions* TV show. Clennott came up with the idea of weekly record hops at Canobie in the early 1960s. It wasn't long before she and disk jockey Dave Maynard, (shown at right in 1965) were on stage every Friday night spinning platters and introducing Top-40 stars.

Some things, like the dress code requiring coats and ties for men, remained the same. And small ads announcing the weekend's performers still appeared in Thursday newspapers, just as they had in the '30s and '40s—only now the names were Gene Pitney, Herman's Hermits, Little Anthony, the Kingsmen, or Mitch Ryder and the Detroit Wheels. Ticket prices, too, remained reasonable. When the Beach Boys (shown above) appeared on July 6, 1965, tickets sold for as little as $3.

A lucky break brought a crowd of almost 5,300 to Canobie on September 3, 1965, blocking up roads near the park for hours. Early that year, two unknowns, Sonny and Cher, contracted to perform in August, for the small sum of $2,500 plus a percentage. When the date came, they were the hottest thing in the music business, with a number-one hit called "I Got You Babe." The William Morris Agency tried to cancel their low-paying Canobie appearance but only succeeded in delaying it a week.

By 1967, the dance hall's days were numbered. The dress code became difficult to enforce, vandalism was a problem at night when the dances let out, and bands were demanding huge fees and special perks that put smaller venues like Canobie out of the bidding. The ballroom closed its doors in 1968 and, except for special occasions, hasn't been used for dancing since.

Five

Living Their Dream

The 1950s were particularly hard on Canobie, with a fire, a hurricane, and a robbery all taking their toll. Other things had happened, too. The big bands that drew so many to the park were now all but gone, and amusement parks in general were on the decline. Whereas there had once been more than 2,000 roller coasters in the country, there were now only about 200. Finally, in March of 1958, the Hollands sold Canobie. The buyers were three close friends and neighbors from Cliffside Park, New Jersey—Claude "Lou" Captell, Kazmir Ulaky, and Anthony Berni (above). For them, the purchase of an amusement park was the realization of a dream.

Canobie's buyers were veteran amusement concessionaires. The Ulakys ran Skee Ball at New Jersey's Palisades Park and, for several Christmas seasons, had a kiddie ride inside Macy's main store. Berni had Pokerino at Palisades, and Captell's concessions at Norumbega in Newton, Massachusetts, included this Canobie sportscar ride (above). When they decided to put everything on the line and buy a park of their own, they considered two. Rocky Glenn Park in Pennsylvania lost out to Canobie. Salem's proximity to Boston and its soon-to-be-built Interstate 93 closed the $450,000 deal. The men may have soon wondered what they were in for. On their first stay at the park's caretaker house, a blizzard hit and the furnace went out. To keep warm, Lou and Kaz burned bowling pins gathered from the alleys in the back of the building shown below. Updating the fun house portion of the building to this look was one of their first projects.

The new owners' inaugural season in 1958 opened with seven Sundays of rain. Inundated with mud, they desperately lined the park's dirt paths with 6'-by-6' steel plates. Two years later, the three men spread, raked, and rolled hot top themselves, to create Canobie's first paved walkways.

More changes and improvements were made every year, such as the purchase of cube-cluster street lights (opposite page) from the 1964/65 New York World's Fair. New concessions were added, too. Paintin' Place, a spin-paint concession, was very popular during the '60s and '70s. It was fun squirting colors onto the spinning card—until you had to carry the wet, sticky mess around with you!

First operated by the Hollands, this military Duck boat ride was inherited by the new owners. They kept it in use for a few years until the *Canobie Queen* pontoon boat was launched. A knack for spotting trends in the amusement industry enabled the Bernis, the Ulakys, and the Captells to continually keep the park fresh and exciting. In fact, by Canobie's seventy-fifth anniversary, it enjoyed the same four-star rating as Walt Disney World in Florida.

This modern entrance sign was added in the early 1960s. At about the same time, a billboard, painted by Kaz Ulaky, stood on the roof of the old post office in the Depot. The operations of the park were divided among the families, with the Ulakys focusing on promotion, the Bernis managing personnel, and the Captells handling maintenance of rides and buildings. The hands-on involvement of all three families in Canobie's management continues today.

What more fitting end to the story of Canobie Lake Park than a final peek at its most popular ride? Now dubbed the Yankee Canonball, the state's only surviving wooden coaster is rated as one of the nation's ten best by the American Coaster Enthusiasts organization. And, like the roller coaster, Canobie Lake Park is still going strong. Happy memories live in the hearts of millions who have passed through her stone pillars.

Six

The Little Country Track

Rockingham Park holds a fascinating history—little known to most of us, yet bearing national scope and effect. At a time when many states were outlawing gambling on horse racing, two famous and wildly successful Wall Streeters, John W. Gates and August Belmont II, were looking for a place to build a track similar to the renowned Saratoga. With its rural setting, easy rail access from Boston, and—most importantly—its location in a state where gambling on horses wasn't yet explicitly illegal, Salem seemed like the perfect spot. It was here that Belmont and Gates would build their "little country track by the side of the road."

Gates was a former barbed-wire salesman whose flamboyant willingness to "Bet-a Million" led him to form and control many companies, including the one that became Texaco. He is best remembered, though, for the $2 million he won after laying down the largest bet in racing history—on his own horse, Royal Flush. Belmont, a director of Gates' Louisville & Nashville Railroad, was a major financier and engineer. He built the New York City subway system, the Cape Cod Canal, and New York's Belmont Park. He also bred the famous Man O'War. In 1905, along with investors from the Mellon, Drake, Vanderbilt, and Whitney families, Gates and Belmont put up the money to build Rockingham Park.They purchased 437 acres, including the farms of Charles Kimball and Isaac Woodbury, and began construction of all the necessary facilities, including the clubhouse and grandstand seen below.

As rumors spread that a racetrack was coming to town, Peter LaCourt wasted no time in building a hotel (above) across the street. Called the Venetian Palace, its name was an ironic overstatement in more ways than one. Besides being a lodging house, it was also an agency supplying Italian laborers for construction at Rockingham. It's doubtful that many of those immigrant workers ever actually got to stay at the hotel. As the rare postcard below illustrates, most of them were housed in much less luxurious quarters nearby. As horrific as it seems, sod and shanty communities like this were not uncommon near construction and road-building sites all over the Merrimack Valley. The low-paid, traveling workers couldn't afford other accommodations, so they erected temporary settlements, often including gardens to guarantee themselves enough to eat. The former hotel building still stands today, at 69 South Broadway, several hundred feet south of the post office.

Laborers laid out a one-mile racing oval at Rockingham, with a three-quarter-mile straightaway running north from it almost to Main Street, across Central Street from the Rockingham Hotel. The hotel was enlarged and totally remodeled at the same time, in anticipation of the wealthy crowds expected at the park. This photograph of the renovated building's Central Street side was taken in 1906.

Within just a few months, a million dollars had been invested in Rockingham Park's clubhouse, grandstand, track, stables, and other facilities. At the same time, however, the state Supreme Court had been busy, too—making it clear that no racetrack featuring betting would be allowed to operate in New Hampshire. No one at Rockingham seemed very worried. The Boston & Maine scheduled special trains to bring bettors in from as far away as New York City. The trolley company also prepared—setting aside twenty cars for opening day.

Ten thousand people came to Salem on June 28, 1906, opening day of the scheduled twenty-one-day meet. Greeted by gorgeous weather and the beautiful new grounds, the crowd settled in for an exciting six-race program planned for the afternoon. The first race ever held at Rockingham was won by a two-year-old horse named Alyth, who nipped Killochan at the wire. The winning jockey was Carrol Dade—son of a California Supreme Court justice.

The park had its own private police force. One member is seen here, pausing on Pleasant Street near today's mall entrance. Police were among the many who couldn't believe it when the sheriff showed up on Rockingham's second day—and shut gambling down by the end of the fourth race. The rest of the twenty-one-day meet was completed as a spectator sport. Belmont and Gates abandoned the venture and retreated to New York, leaving the park's builder unpaid.

By 1910, seven years after Kitty Hawk, aviation mania was grabbing hold of Americans as records for speed, altitude, and distance were being shattered. The New England Aviation Company decided that Rockingham's three-quarter-mile straightaway would make an ideal runway. They scheduled an aviation meet there on Columbus Day 1911. Between fifteen and twenty thousand people came to the newly named Rockingham Aviation Park that day. A second air show, held on Thanksgiving, drew only seven hundred—and Rockingham's second life became history.

Pilot James Barry
SPECIAL FLIGHT
MAY 19, 1938
Salem Depot, N. H.
"By the Waters of Canobie Lake"
N.A.M.W.
ROUTE 602001
FIRST OFFICIAL DISPATCH
VIA AEROPLANE, FROM
ROCKINGHAM PARK,
SALEM, N. H. TO
LAWRENCE, MASS.
MAY 30, 1912
David E. Stevens
Postmaster
NATIONAL AIRMAIL WEEK-MAY-15-21,1938
FIRST FLIGHT MAY 19,1938.
LAWRENCE MASS.
THE FRIENDLIEST CITY IN THE UNITED STATES
WEAVES THE WORLDS WORSTEDS
CACHET SPONSORED BY THE
LAWRENCE PHILATELIC SOCIETY
SALEM DEPOT
MAY 19
12 30 PM
1938
TOP
21836
AIR MAIL
6c
U.S. POSTAGE
P.W. HALL
SALEM DEPOT
N.H.

In early 1912, Salem postmaster Fred Buxton petitioned the Postal Department in Washington for permission to try moving mail by airplane. They approved and on May 30, pilot Lincoln Beachey took off from Rockingham Park carrying a pouch of mail postmarked for Lawrence. Interestingly, Salem's government-sanctioned flight preceded Washington's "official" establishment of U.S. airmail service (May 15, 1918), by six years! This commemorative envelope was carried on a reenactment of the flight during National Airmail Week in 1938.

Another group of investors, partially financed by a loan from Methuen millionaire Edward F. Searles, decided to take a gamble on making the park a success. On August 29, 1912, just eighty days after the airmail flight, the first Rockingham Fair opened.

In addition to featuring many contests and World's Fair-type spectacles, $58,500 in prize money was up for grabs in eighteen harness horse races—Salem's first. The Canadian Government and the U.S. Department of Agriculture both put on large displays, and the American Kennel Club ran a dog show. Carnival rides and side games abounded on "Looney Lane."

After rain kept attendance—and profits—down at the 1912 fair, Searles bought a $100,000 rain insurance policy from Lloyds of London for the 1913 expo. As it turned out, though, it would be competition from other fairs that would lower attendance in 1913—and at the next two fairs as well. By 1916, Rockingham's grounds once again lay dormant—and Searles owned the park. He had acquired it by quitclaim in 1915 when its operators defaulted on their loan.

The Rockingham Park Police Department, seen here at the 1914 fair, had been formed back in 1906. Many of its members were off-duty officers from Lawrence. The existence of a private force at the track was one of the factors which led to the original racing venture's demise. When Gates and Belmont's plan to self-police the establishment was included in the company's charter, it raised a few eyebrows in Concord, being seen as a ruse to avoid outside interference.

The park was unused during 1916. The next year, however, its grounds came to life once again when America entered "the war to end all wars," World War I. The United States 14th Army Engineers set up camp on Rockingham's large tract of land adjacent to the railroad—an ideal site for training. These two doughboys, along with the rest of the unit, would soon receive their orders to ship out to France.

After eight idle years, the park roared to life yet again in 1925, when former race car driver Jack LeCain brought auto racing to Rockingham. Pat Holland, who would purchase Canobie Lake Park six years later, got the job of preparing the old horse racing oval for its next incarnation. He also readied a parking lot to accommodate 15,000 cars.

On the Fourth of July, the first of several major auto races was waged on Salem's soon-to-be famous auto track. The inaugural event was a 100-mile race—100 laps around the oval. The grueling competition was won by Ralph DePalma, averaging an astounding 76.9 miles per hour.

ROCKINGHAM MOTOR SPEEDWAY INC

SAT. OCT. 17 1925 2 P.M.

NATIONAL AUTUMN CLASSIC

Speedway Manager

ADMIT TO ONE SEAT

General Admission	$2.00
Reserved Seat	5.00
Tax Paid	.70
TOTAL	$7.70

TREMONT PRESS, BOSTON

In event of postponement ticket will be honored on postponed date. NO MONEY REFUNDED

RAIN CHECK

SAT. OCT. 17

TOTAL PRICE $7.70

ROCKINGHAM MOTOR SPEEDWAY

BOX 13 B 1

SECT. SEAT

GRAND STAND A

Forty thousand people were on hand to see DePalma's win. Other events were held that day, too, including motorcycle races of shorter lengths. The day was such a huge success that plans were immediately put into motion to put Rockingham on a level with the already famous auto track in Indianapolis.

Based on the success of the July Fourth event on the dirt track, 800 men spent the next three months building a giant board track above the oval. Its construction consumed 53 tons of 30-penny nails and one million board feet of spruce lumber—enough lumber to house a town of 1,200 people! It would be one of only twenty-five such wooden bowls in the country—and, at a cost of around $500,000, it would be the finest. Grandstand capacity was increased from 5,800 to 12,064 and infield seating was added to hold another 8,000.

The corners were built to a 49 degree angle, the steepest in the nation. Cars had to sustain speeds of at least 118 mph to avoid tumbling off the track into the infield. The behemoth structure was 6,602 feet around and 60 feet wide. Opening day was planned for Columbus Day 1925, but rain and other mishaps delayed it until October 31. A total of sixteen cars had qualified for the 250-mile main event. Peter DePaolo, who had won Indy that year, won Rockingham in 1:59:13.6, taking the $9,000 first prize. His yellow Duesenberg had averaged 125.2 mph.

Peter DePaolo (left) never left a starting line without his baby shoes tied to his car's front spring. They were certainly lucky for him in 1925—not only was he world champion, but he also was the first driver ever to average more than 100 mph at the Indianapolis 500, a record that wouldn't be broken until 1932.

The field at Rockingham always included a list of world-famous drivers, and fans came by the thousands to watch them battle it out. Harry Hartz, Vic Spooner, Tommy Milton, Frank Lockhart, Earl Cooper, and Leon Duray all raced at the track. Even a young Derren Vartanian of Salem—who had helped DePaolo's crew in 1925—became a racer at Rockingham and elsewhere.

By 1929 the board track was falling apart. Carpenters were even working under it during races, popping up between cars to patch holes. It was a futile effort. Drivers were taking splinters and knots in the face and deadly accidents were becoming an epidemic. In September, the Lowell Building Wrecking Company disassembled the track. Auto racing resumed on the dirt oval periodically until 1932.

Seven

The Lou Smith Revival

Auto racing proved that Rockingham could draw huge crowds and big money. Salem's potential caught the eye of Lou Smith, the promoter and horse racing enthusiast who, in 1928, built King's Park in Montreal. In 1930, Smith's potential caught the eye of Salem, a town anxious for any opportunities that a permanent establishment at Rockingham might bring. The Lions Club invited Smith to a meeting at the Rockingham Hotel that year to hear what he had in mind. With an ability to gain the support of politicians and a knack for promotion, Smith—shown above with comedian Jimmy Durante in 1954—was just what Salem had been waiting for. Rockingham would soon become the first legal thoroughbred track in New England.

By the spring of 1931, Smith and his investors had formed the New Hampshire Breeders Association and an almost $200,000 face-lift was underway at Rockingham. The old horse stables were repaired and new ones were added. The grandstand (above in 1933), clubhouse, and administration building were all painted and polished up. Horse racing was returning to Salem in grand style! Of course, gambling on races was still illegal but, amazingly, that didn't seem to bother anyone. Many public officials were in the crowd of 15,000 on July 1, 1931 for this latest "first day" of racing. No complaints were heard.

Area residents had fun, good-paying jobs to fend off the depression, trains and autos packed with itchy-fingered bettors were streaming in, and Smith was thrilled. Everyone was happy, it seemed, but the sheriff—who, with his men, had spent opening day quietly gathering evidence against the operation. Just as in 1906, the place was shut down on day two! Smith recruited several influential Salemites, including Selectman William T. Barron. By 1933, with the promise of huge revenues to state coffers, they succeeded in getting pari-mutuel betting legalized once and for all. On June 21, 1933, racing again began in Salem.

Now enjoying a successful, totally legal operation, Lou Smith was the big-time promoter he had worked so hard to become. He loved to rub elbows with well-known people and never missed a photo opportunity—like this one with Joe Kennedy Jr. in the '30s. Even a partial list of visitors to "The Rock" over the years is impressive: Damon Runyan, Al Jolson, Ruby Keeler, Judy Garland, Ronald Coleman, Gloria Swanson, Charlie Chaplin, Eddie Cantor, and Louis B. Mayer.

As a teenager, Smith managed and promoted fights and was even a boxer himself. In 1937, Rockingham announced plans to start a training program for young men with heavyweight-championship potential. No topflight talent turned up, but former champion Jack Dempsey did. He posed for this photo with Lou's wife, Lutza, during his visit.

Lou was famous for charity fund-raising promotions at "the Rock," and he put his skills to use for the war effort in the '40s, starting even before Pearl Harbor. Smith offered free admission to anyone bringing aluminum pots and pans to the turnstiles on opening day in 1941. From then until the war ended, he came up with idea after idea. Special races run to benefit the National War Relief Fund alone raised a total of more than $282,000.

Horse racing can be risky business, as evidenced by these jockeys recovering from a nasty spill. Nurse Clara Johnston and attendant Roger Lambert provided the care for jockeys Sconza, Farrell, and Emery. Jockeys weren't the only ones injured at the track over the years. In 1934, a horse named Spring Steel collapsed and died during a race at Rockingham. Spring Steel's owner arranged to have him buried in the infield of the oval—headstone and all—where he remains today.

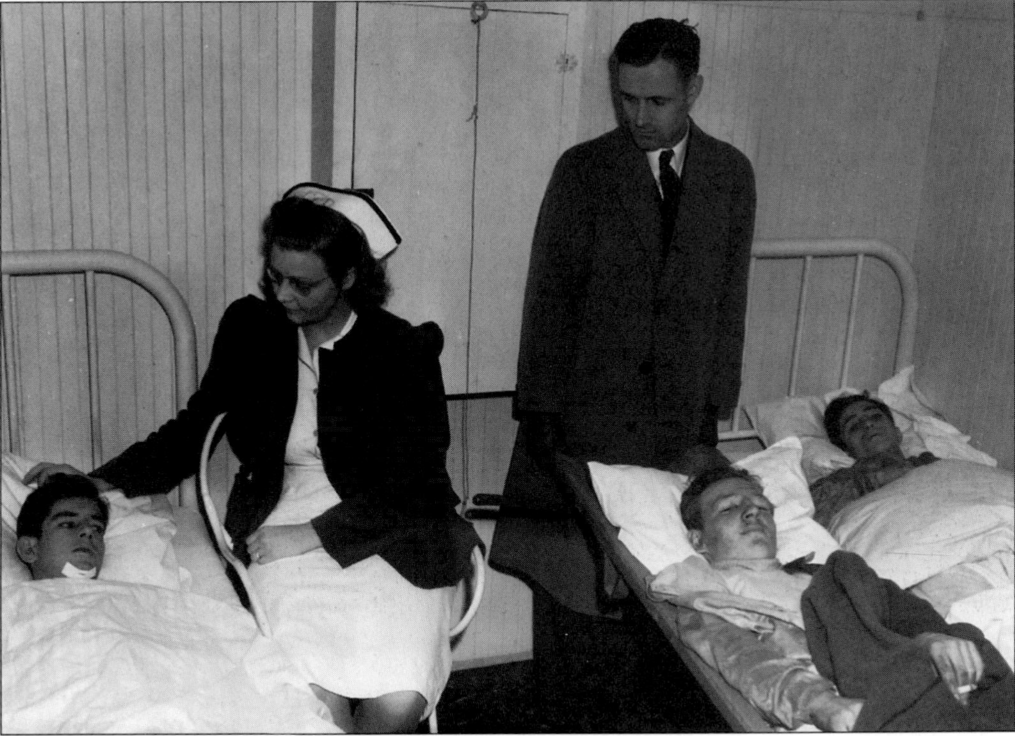

Lou loved every minute of his life in Salem and had plenty of fun in his 400-acre backyard. As a young teenager, he left his hometown of Passaic, New Jersey, by running away with a circus. Reverting back to those circus years, Smith offered a bale of hay as a prize if he failed to guess the weight of horse and rider within fifty pounds. That was his clever and flamboyant way of showing off his new Fairbanks Morse scales to the press.

Always one for a promotional gimmick, Smith brought in plow horses from county fairs all over New Hampshire for 1948's first annual Plow Horse Derby. The non-betting derby was an annual event for a decade or more. The October 1949 half-mile race was won by North Salem resident Donald Taylor (above), who rode his horse Buster to victory.

Constantly willing to help a good cause, "Uncle Lou," as he was affectionately called, provided space for Pelham New Hampshire's St. Patrick's Parish to raffle this 1948 Chevy as part of the church's September Carnival festivities.

Besides the Plow Horse Derby, many other wacky races were held over the years. From 1941 through the late 1950s, female rodeo contestants came up from Boston Garden for the Gene Autrey and Roy Rogers Cowgirl Races—a perennial hit with the fans. 1944 brought the Grandpappy Special, in which the horses were all ridden by old-time jockeys. But the most unusual of all Smith's gimmick races was, without a doubt, the ostrich race of Saturday, October 28, 1950!

As they had for virtually every event at the park since 1906, crowds from Boston and points south arrived for racing via the Boston & Maine. Extra trains were scheduled by the railroad for weekends, holidays, and special events. Rail service to the track was briefly curtailed in the early years of World War II, hurting both Rockingham and the B&M. The rails left the main line and entered Rockingham through still-existing gates in the chain link fence across Route 28 from today's post office. The siding then looped around the radius of the racing oval, and ended in a southerly direction in front of the administration building, just north of the grandstand. In the heyday of the railroads, trains not only brought racing fans to the park—they also brought horses, grooms, jockeys, hay, feed, and many other necessities.

After fifty-six years of rail service to Rockingham—both steam and diesel—trains from Boston's North Station were finally discontinued in 1962. The park's rails were taken up and the Rockingham Racer was no more. The space was then promoted as Rockingham's new Bus Gate, and it was used for that purpose well into the last years of the Smith dynasty.

A flurry of activity and anticipation stirred through Salem as each year's meet drew closer. Trailer after trailer, carrying thoroughbreds and their grooms, thundered up South Broadway and rolled through the main gates on Route 28, across from today's post office. At Rockingham's peak in the mid-1960s, over 1,200 horses were stabled at the park every summer.

A black gelding named Brass Monkey ran his way into the hearts of Rock fans in the 1930s. The $1,000 claiming horse had the uncanny ability to run dead last for most of the race—then break wide open to win by a nose. For five years he won race after race with the same ploy. After becoming almost a cult figure at the track, he was guest of honor at this retirement party thrown for him at Boston's ill-fated Coconut Grove nightclub.

In 1947, more than fifty of the horses stabled at Rockingham were stricken with swamp fever. Smith immediately isolated the sick animals in these quarantine tents. Almost sixty horses succumbed, but Smith's quick action saved over a thousand others that were at risk. As a result, he was credited with saving thoroughbred racing in New England. That September, Rockingham ran an emergency nineteen-day meet to help horse owners recoup some of their losses.

Salem loved Lou. He had offered townspeople the chance to get out of the depression and they took it, by voting 617 to 2 in favor of racing at the special town meeting called in 1933. From the beginning, he pledged to hire as many New Hampshire workers as he could. Rockingham brought lots of jobs to lots of people—as ticket sellers (at right in 1950), policemen, cashiers, food workers, maintenance people, horse walkers, parking lot attendants, newspaper vendors and more.

The press room was a hot spot of activity as reporters rattled out exciting copy describing the play by play of each race. Stories from the Rock went out over the wire, by teletype, directly from reporters' keyboards to major newspapers and wire services all over the country. In 1958, the press box was enlarged to keep up with the growing success of the park.

One ill-conceived idea, in the late 1940s, was to cover races by helicopter. One would think that the noise of the chopper might scare the horses a bit. Well, spook them it did, and it drowned out the announcer's voice, too. Needless to say, the experiment lasted just this one day.

This c. 1964 aerial photo is more significant for what isn't there than for what is. At right, there is no Veterans Memorial Parkway across Route 28 from Rockingham Boulevard. There are no malls or shopping plazas, either. In fact, most of the businesses on the east side of Route 28 opposite the track aren't there yet. At the left end of the racing oval, the Ole Rock Drive-in Theater sits across South Broadway. Inside the big oval is the half-mile harness track.

Although harness racing appeared at the Rockingham Fairs in 1912 through 1915, it wasn't until 1958 that the wheels really started to spin, so to speak. A half-mile clay track for sulkies was constructed inside the big oval, sharing the existing track's home stretch (see aerial photo p. 118). Spring and fall trotter meets were held at the Rock until 1980.

At the end of the spring harness races, and again at the end of the flats in the fall, men, trucks, and tractors worked twenty-four hours a day for three days. Thousands of yards of clay for the sulkies—or soft, screened loam for the "runners," needed to be scraped up, moved and replaced to accommodate the opening of the next meet a few days later.

New for 1956 was Smith's million dollar clubhouse. The beautiful glass and stainless steel structure, with its curved facade, was the talk of the town—and the racing world.

Featuring Salem's first escalator and a stunning staircase that seemed suspended in mid-air, the new clubhouse brought the Rock to a level of class that put it on par with the country's finest tracks.

The unveiling of the sensational new clubhouse on opening day of the 1956 meet brought with it a new attendance record—bettering the old record by almost 3,000 people. One of the most talked about features of the building was this modernistic suspended stairway.

The Track Kitchen was a center of park activity, even on Thanksgiving in 1959 when the venerable old promoter donned a chef's hat for the camera. The cafeteria-style restaurant came to life well before dawn during racing seasons, serving up a hot, hearty breakfast for the hundreds of grooms, jockeys, trainers and other track workers who filed through the place every day. Outsiders were welcome, too. Long lines like the one below, photographed in 1963, formed out in the parking lot on Labor Day between morning and afternoon races. The restaurant was operated by the Clarence Hockridge family from 1933 to 1980. Hand-painted murals lined its knotty-pine walls, depicting racing records set at Rockingham. Upstairs, a dormitory housed kitchen personnel, some of whom worked for Hockridge for forty years. The Track Kitchen has been closed to the general public since 1980.

Motels, trailer parks, and restaurants sprang up in Salem to serve the influx of workers and vacationers coming to Rockingham. One of the first was The Birches, started as a restaurant by Arthur and Evelyn Seed in 1929. When horse racing began, tourist cabins were built behind the restaurant at the corner of Hampshire Road and Route 28. Requests for trailer spaces in the late '30s led them to add those, too. The couple on the right in the *c.* 1953 photo above came by train or bus from Brooklyn, New York, for thirty-six consecutive summers. Three generations worked at The Birches, and generations of other Salem families worked at the track itself. In the photo of clubhouse waitresses below, Yvonne Greenwood is second from the left. Her mother, daughters, and son all worked at Rockingham, too. Others in the picture are, left to right: Ann Foize, Theresa Bileveau, unknown, and Helen Bach.

Lou Smith's successes at Rockingham included many firsts in New England racing. Foremost was legalized pari-mutuel betting in 1933. Two years later he started jockey insurance, and in 1936 instituted daily doubles.

The 1940s brought double headers—two full racing programs in the same day. In 1952 he introduced the New England Futurity, an annual race exclusively for New England-bred two-year-olds. The 1960s were full of new wagering possibilities as Smith first unveiled PIC SIX, then twin doubles and perfectas.

In the jockey room, these riders passed the time between races, waiting for their turn in the saddle. Jockeys, grooms and hot-walkers also had baseball teams and boxing matches. Favorite jockeys abounded during Smith's years: Willie Shoemaker, Eddie Arcaro, Earl Porter, John Longden, Tony DeSpirito, Jackie Westrope, Norman Mercier, Leroy Moyers, and so many more. Tragedy struck when Henry Wajda, a long-time favorite at Rockingham, was killed during a race on the track.

A non-English-speaking Russian immigrant at twenty-three, Sam Simons finally saved $8,000. With it, he became hot dog concessionaire at Boston Arena. By 1928 he had parlayed his original sum into enough to become food service provider at Boston Garden. Since the Garden sponsored auto races at Rockingham, Simons got to know its potential. He worked closely with Lou Smith in getting the park and legalized racing established, then provided food services at the Rock for years.

The Smiths became close friends with Boston's Richard Cardinal Cushing. He often visited Rockingham, staying in their apartment on the top floor of the administrative building. With its porch looking out over the park to the horizon beyond, it must have been a little bit of heaven. Lutza Smith (seated, right) raised millions for the Crippled Children's Non-Sectarian Fund at field days like this, with Cardinal Cushing usually celebrating Mass under a canopy set up at the finish line.

Babe Rubenstein was the "Voice of Rockingham" for many years. During the 1938 hurricane, he nearly lost his life when the broadcasting booth almost blew off the roof of the grandstand. Just before the finish of that day's second race, the nation's leading rider, Warren Yarberry, had a close call, too. He was blown off his mount by the fierce winds. The rest of the program was canceled but, despite considerable damage to the park, racing resumed the very next day.

The track photographer was always busy, taking promotional and winner's circle photos, as well as the great "thundering hooves" action shots we all associate with horse racing. In 1952, Smith saw action photos taken at a Rhode Island track by Tony Conte (above). He was so impressed with them that he asked Conte to do some work at Rockingham. Conte did—for about forty years. Many of the photos in this chapter were taken by Tony or his predecessor, Meyer Ostroff.

Douglas W. Seed
(NAME)
223 Main St.
(NUMBER AND STREET)
Salem, NH.
(CITY) PLEASE PRINT (STATE)

STATE OF NEW HAMPSHIRE
1st SWEEPSTAKES RACE
SEPTEMBER, 1964

THIS IS ONLY AN ACKNOWLEDGMENT OF PURCHASE. IT NEED NOT BE RETAINED OR PRESENTED FOR PAYMENT. PRIZES WILL BE AWARDED ON THE BASIS OF THE NAME AND ADDRESS ON EACH WINNING SWEEPSTAKES TICKET IN POSSESSION OF NEW HAMPSHIRE SWEEPSTAKES COMMISSION.

1473483

NON-SALEABLE — NON TRANSFERABLE
NET PROCEEDS TO PUBLIC EDUCATION

John W. King GOVERNOR

NEW HAMPSHIRE SWEEPSTAKES COMMISSION

Edward J. Powers EXECUTIVE DIRECTOR — Henry J. Turcotte COMMISSIONER

Howell F. Shepard CHAIRMAN — Edward Sanel COMMISSIONER

In search of new revenues, the 1963 New Hampshire Legislature authorized the nation's first legal lottery in more than fifty years. The 1964 New Hampshire Sweepstakes set the precedent for the state lotteries Americans enjoy today. Using a system similar to the Irish Sweepstakes, each ticket was matched to one of 300 horses nominated to run in a special sweepstakes race. Tickets were sold off-track, at special sweepstakes booths and state liquor stores. Almost two million tickets were sold, at a price of three dollars each. Half the money went to education. Odds of winning a prize ranging from $200 to $100,000 were 1,000 to 1. This ticket—a loser—is the author's souvenir of September 12, 1964.

Lou Smith looked on as Governor John W. King, with the aid of 1964's Miss New Hampshire, picked one of six grand-prize-winning tickets in the state's first sweepstakes race. Roman Brother was the winning horse and six lucky people each won $100,000. None of the winners chosen were from New England.

Throngs of people were expected to descend on Salem for the big race. The track spent $20,000 just on additional parking space. They also built the $65,000 high-tech retractable bridge seen above, to move the planned overflow crowd into the oval's infield. The town called in extra police and fire units, and a helicopter was hired for traffic control. The media publicized every preparation and expectation so heavily that, when race day came, only 17,000 people dared to show up!

Attendance may have been a bust, but souvenirs abounded and the race was nationally televised—a first for Salem. Sweepstakes races continued through 1967. Lou Smith was still leading his beloved Rockingham at the time of his death on April 19, 1969.

On another sad day, in 1980, the grandstand went up in multi-million dollar flames. Unable to recover from the loss, the park sat idle for three years until it was sold to Rockingham Venture, Inc., the firm that operates it today.

Acknowledgments

Special thanks to the following, who unselfishly provided the authors with their knowledge and with unlimited access to their collections: O. R. Cummings,Trolleys of the Mass. Northeastern; Anthony Conte, Rockingham Park collection; Maurice Holland Jr., The Holland family collection; Salem Historical Society; Lester Hall, The Hall family collection; Edward Callahan, Rockingham Park general manager; James A. Sayer Jr.; and Jack Lahey, one of the area's premier postcard collectors.

The authors also wish to thank the following individuals, organizations, and businesses who have provided photographs or invaluable assistance for this book: Mary Seed, Wayne Ulaky, Mr. and Mrs. Kazmir Ulaky, David Cook, Tom Morrow, Scott Hills, Suzanne McHugh Piscitello, Canobie Lake Park, Paul Larochelle, Louise Ackerman, Ernest Mack, Ken Skulski, Carol McShane, Charles Wolfe, Jeff Barraclough, Methuen Historical Commission, Guy Ackerman, James Falls, Stephanie Micklon, Christine Willis, Yvonne Greenwood, Ruth Clenott, WBZ Radio, Donald Boland, Rich DeMerle, The Lawrence Eagle Tribune, Arthur Mueller, The Salem Observer, Pauline Keith, Thomas Grassi, Margaret Robbins, Margaret Holland, Mr. and Mrs. Carl Braun III, Margaret Hepworth, George J. Khoury, Rockingham Venture, Inc., Immigrant City Archives, Buddy Winiarz, Fred Barone, Tom Ippolito, The Lundberg Family, Mr. and Mrs. Daniel Donabedian, Ruth Bourdelais, Mr. and Mrs. Clarence Hockridge Jr., Francis D. Sangermano, Frank J. Leone Jr., Mr. and Mrs. Robert D. Goundrey, Jill Goundrey Moe, Ruth Henning, Tina Gagnon, Joan Shonenberger, Spectrum Business Service, Steve Barbin, Lawence Public Library, Kelley Library, Paul Garabedian Jr., Lynne Snierson, Jim Forzese, Ted Herbert, James M. Smith, Margaret Russell, Richard Noyes, Theresa Di Pippo, New Hampshire Good Roads Association, Martin J. McDonough Jr., St. Joseph's Parish, and Marjorie Jackson.

This book is lovingly dedicated to the authors' father, Douglas A. Seed (1915–1995), a life-long resident of Salem, whose love of his hometown and memories of the trolleys, Canobie Lake Park, and Rockingham Park were the inspiration for this work.